# READING
# BETWEEN ▶
# THE LINES

# READING
# BETWEEN ▶
# THE LINES

## Improve Your Scores
## on English &
## Social Studies Tests

Barbara Dallon
*and*
Wendy Ratner

LEARNINGEXPRESS

NEW YORK

Library of Congress Cataloging-in-Publication Data:
Dallon, Barbara.
    Reading between the lines : a student's guide to improving scores on English & social studies
tests / by Barbara Dallon and Wendy Ratner.—1st ed.
        p. cm.
    ISBN 1-57685-415-9 (pbk. : alk. paper)
    1. Test-taking skills—Handbooks, manuals, etc.  2. English language—Composition and exer-
cises—Examinations—Study guides.  3. Social sciences—Examinations—Study guides.  I. Ratner,
Wendy. II. Title.
    LB3060.57 .D35 2002
    371.26—dc21
                                                                            2002003278

Printed in the United States of America
9 8 7 6 5 4 3 2 1
First Edition

ISBN 1-57685-415-9

For more information or to place an order, contact LearningExpress at:
    900 Broadway
    Suite 604
    New York, NY 10003

Or visit us at:
    www.learnatest.com

# Acknowledgments

We have included many of our primary source documents with the kind permission of HistoryCentral.com. We highly recommend that you visit this site for accessing primary source documents.

# Contents

Contents

# Introduction

## DEAR STUDENT,

What do Britney Spears, N'Sync, Michael Jordan, The Rock, Oprah Winfrey, J.K. Rowling, and Bill Gates have in common? They are able to entertain, compete, write, compose, or invent better than most, and are outstanding in their different fields. Each has developed an individual method to achieve excellence in what they do. We do not see the behind-the-scenes hard work these stars have done nor do we see the help and support given them by their parents, teachers, coaches, consultants, and crews who help them succeed. Although this book is not intended to turn you into the next professional star, it is designed to help you understand, practice, and write effective responses to DBQs (Document-Based Questions) so that you may improve your scores on standardized tests and become a more successful student. It is important to read and review each chapter in sequence in order to gain the full benefit of the teaching strategies given to you.

If you are in middle school or high school, using the strategies in this book can help you prepare for state exams. Most students in middle schools and high schools will have to answer document-based questions in their social studies tests and on their state assessment exams. Even teachers of high school advanced placement social studies classes expect their students to write effective answers to document-based questions.

By writing an effective document-based essay, you will demonstrate your ability to be a successful, informative author, as well as an interpretive, analytical historian. The job of a historian is to study the causes and effects of past events. When you begin to examine and interpret primary source documents, you are acting as a historian. It is your job to put the pieces of the history puzzle together to come out with an accurate, informative conclusion. The job of an author is to accurately inform the reader in an interesting and enlightening manner. By writing your essay, you will inform the reader of the historical position you are taking. You will use the primary source documents to support your position. The more appealing and enlightening the essay, the higher your score will be on the assessment.

You can use this book to learn how to write great document-based essays. As you learn to master the skills in this book, you will be better prepared to organize and develop essays that you must write for homework as well as in-class tests. It will also improve your reading and thinking skills. These skills will help you throughout your school career and will last a lifetime, whether or not you become the next Britney Spears or Michael Jordan.

## DEAR PARENT,

The writers of this book are parents, as well as teachers. We have sat at the kitchen table countless nights wondering just how much help should we give our kids. Are we saying the right things or not enough? Are we encouraging our children or making their lives more difficult? No doubt about it—school is more difficult for present-day students than it was just a few years ago. Higher standards, newly developed requirements, and exams have placed extra stresses on our children and on us. We would like to offer some suggestions, not as teachers, but as the parents of our own children who are going through the same uncharted waters as your children.

Suggestions from two moms who have been there:

1. Be calm. Frustrated parents can frustrate their children. For some, the learning process is long and difficult. Let your child know that achieving a proper outcome takes hard work, time, and patience.
2. Do fun things together. The learning experience should be one of fun and laughter. Try to encourage learning by targeting your child's interests.
3. Balance doing and guiding. We are our children's best advocate, but sometimes guiding can turn into doing. Be sure that it is the child who is *doing* the work and the parent who is *guiding* the child through the work. We cannot always be there for our children. It is important that we offer as much guidance as possible without actually doing the work for them.
4. Play. Children should lead playful, active lives. Try to encourage learning by playing. Computer games and family games can offer great support in a child's education.
5. Eat. Healthy children who receive the proper nutrition become better students. Be sure that before going to school or taking an exam, your child has eaten a healthy meal.
6. Reward. Give your child a sense of accomplishment by rewarding them for a job well done. Rewards do not have to be elaborate, but you should show gratitude for their hard work.
7. Learn together. Children are more responsive when the learning process is shared. They enjoy watching their parents learn along with them. They no longer feel isolated as a student, but begin to view the learning process as one which lasts a lifetime.
8. Be positive. Positive reinforcement and a positive attitude will encourage your child to continue on, no matter how stressful the situation may seem.
9. Support your child's teacher. Consistency at home and school will lead to a positive relationship between you and your son or daughter's teacher. Consistency will reinforce learned concepts and will help guide your child toward educational success. Familiarize yourself with the teacher's class and homework procedures. Talk about your child's progress with the teacher at conference time. Follow up with phone conferences if you have questions or need advice.

10. Be informed about requirements and state exams. Understand the many challenges facing your child today. By familiarizing yourself with curriculum requirements and state exams, you will be better able to help your child prepare.

11. Get sample copies of exams. Practice makes perfect. The more your child practices taking these exams, the better his or her test-taking strategies will become.

12. Talk to your child. Find out what he or she thinks his or her strengths and weaknesses are. What does your child feel comfortable with? Where does he or she feel he or she needs to improve? In order to help our children, we must first understand where they need help.

13. Lead your son or daughter to independent learning. Children need to know how to use the resources around them. Help them learn how to use these resources to become successful students.

14. Have learning conversations. Discover the knowledge your child possesses. How familiar is your child with what is expected of him or her? What can we do to help children acquire the knowledge they need to be successful?

15. Know when to call it a night. Though we live in a fast-paced society where everyone's schedule is busy, we need to learn to appropriately balance our children's activities. Quantity does not necessarily constitute quality. Children who are overtired should not continue working. Develop a study schedule that is appropriate for you and your child. Allow for breaks between sessions. Never allow a child to work until exhaustion sets in!

16. Don't expect perfection. No one is perfect, especially a child. The purpose of making a mistake is to learn from it. Set reasonable expectations and goals for your child. The way for your child to attain success is by feeling successful.

The more support and encouragement we can give our children, the more successful they will be. Let them know that mistakes are acceptable—the road to success is paved with many of them. Remind your kids that by learning from their mistakes and practicing proper study habits, they can and will become successful students. We hope that you will find this book helpful in preparing your child for the vigorous road ahead.

# READING
## BETWEEN ▶
# THE LINES

# DBQs: What Are They?

 his section describes what document-based questions are, states concepts you will need to learn in order to understand these type of questions, and explains the importance of learning to write these types of essays. The bold-faced words are important terms that are defined in the glossary. These terms need to become part of your vocabulary if you are truly going to understand document-based questions.

*Document-Based Questions (DBQs)* are essay questions that ask you to read **primary source documents** in order to answer questions about a topic in history. You may be asked to read, analyze, and interpret news articles, diaries, speeches, photographs, laws, maps, graphs, letters, or cartoons. Any type of original printed material may be used.

## ▶ FAQs (FREQUENTLY ASKED QUESTIONS)

**Did you ever think of yourself as a historian (one who studies history)?**
By reading and interpreting these questions, you actually become an historian. As a historian you will examine historical primary-source writing and then form an opinion on the topic. You must use these documents in your essay to prove your position (**point of view**) on that particular topic.

**Did you ever think of yourself as an author?**

By answering the document-based question, you become an author.

You will write an explanatory essay in which you develop and prove your position on a particular historical topic.

As an author/historian, you must interpret the *validity* of these documents when deciding your position on the topic. In other words, you must read between the lines and figure out if the writer is slanting the truth a certain way because of his or her *bias*.

**Why do your teachers expect you to be able to write an essay answering a DBQ?**

Teachers don't intentionally make life difficult for you. Teachers use the DBQ as a tool to assess your ability to make *inferences* (reading between the lines to get at the writer's true meaning) to help you draw conclusions. This is called *interpreting* a document. Reading for meaning and understanding is essential for you to be a successful student in all your subjects. So, you see why we want to help you succeed.

**How will your mastery of DBQs help you in life?**

Mastering the reading and writing skills for this kind of essay will also prepare you for understanding written material as an adult. (This may include reading the newspaper, a magazine, advertisement, contract, or application.) Every day you are bombarded with the written word. From political leaflets to advertisements, you must make quick decisions about what you read. You must determine who the writer is, what the writer's purpose is, and if you support or disagree with the writer's point of view. Understanding DBQs helps you do that.

# A Glossary of DBQ Terms

his glossary contains a list of terms and definitions that you should know when you tackle any DBQ. Use this checklist to help you study them.

✔ Check the words you already know.
✔ Review the words that sound unfamiliar to you.
✔ Get together with a friend or adult who can help you review these words.
✔ Tape record the words and their meanings and listen to it.
✔ Write or type each word, its meaning, and your own example.
✔ Find examples of the words using excerpts from a magazine or newspaper. Highlight and label the word in the excerpt.

**Bias:** a writer or reader's viewpoint
**Body:** the middle paragraphs of an essay that develop and support the thesis statement
**Conclusion:** the last paragraph of the essay that summarizes the writer's main points and that support the thesis statement
**Document-Based Question (DBQ):** a question on a particular theme or topic that consists of at least five primary source documents that relate to the question or topic

**Essay:** a literary, analytical composition expressing the writer's viewpoint on a single subject

**Historical Context:** historical background information relating to the theme

**Hook:** a captivating sentence or phrase that draws the reader into the reading

**Inference:** a conclusion the reader comes to by using *context clues* (reading between the lines) to get at the true meaning of the text

**Insight:** the ability to gain knowledge and make connections between what one already knows and has experienced (prior knowledge) to what one reads

**Interpret:** to analyze and understand the importance of quotations and events in a particular historical context

**Introductory Paragraph:** the first paragraph of an essay that must include the topic of the essay and the author's opinion on the topic

**Outside Information:** prior knowledge you have about the theme or topic

**Point of View:** the writer's ideas about what happened, the importance of certain people, the motives behind various actions, and the significance of each event

**Primary Source Documents:** documents that come from an original or first source, including journals, speeches, artwork, graphs, and charts

**Scaffolding Questions:** questions associated with each primary source document. Each scaffolding question becomes more difficult than the next.

**Task:** a question or statement about the theme of the DBQ, informing the student of the information he will be required to include in the DBQ and directly relating to the theme

**Theme:** the topic or main idea of the DBQ

**Thesis Statement:** a statement that informs the reader of the main idea of the essay which can be formed by using the documents to answer the question or statement given in the task

**Transition Words:** words that help you connect paragraphs

**Validity:** the strength of a point of view

# Parts of a DBQ

The DBQ includes six important elements or parts that will help you complete your task. The six parts of a DBQ are:

1. Theme
2. Historical Context
3. Task Question
4. Thesis Statement
5. Primary Source Documents
6. Scaffolding Questions

Let's go through each part, step-by-step, using the American Revolution as a theme:

1. **Theme:** The American Revolution
2. **Historical Context:** The historical context provides you with background information relating to the theme. (In this case, it is the American Revolution.) You can use this information to help you gain insight into the theme. Also, the background information can help you write the introduction to your essay.

Example of historical context:

> After the French and Indian War, the American colonists encountered a series of events as a result of rulings handed down from the British Parliament. These proceedings included the Proclamation of 1763, Stamp Act, Sugar Act, Quartering Act, the Townshend Acts, and the Boston Massacre. King George, along with the British Parliament, justified these actions claiming the need for the American colonists to pay for the debt caused by the war. The American colonists believed this was an infringement of their rights since they had no vote in Parliament. They did not believe that Parliament was justified in its actions. After several unsuccessful attempts to reach a settlement with Parliament, the American colonists believed the only solution to the problem was to rebel and break away from Great Britain.

3. **Task Question:** The task question is the actual essay question that you are expected to answer. The task question is directly related to the theme of the essay.

Example of a Task Question:

> Using the information from the documents and your knowledge of Social Studies, write an essay in which you explain whether or not the American colonists were justified in breaking away from Great Britain.

> **Explain:** When you explain a topic, you must make a general statement that shows you understand the concept in the question. Then you must support your main idea with examples, facts, details, and reasons that show how or why something happened. In this case you must interpret documents to determine what your opinion is about whether or not the American colonists were right in separating from Great Britain. Then you must develop an essay clearly stating your point of view, giving many facts and reasons to support your position.

4. **Thesis Statement:** The thesis statement is a sentence that clearly tells the reader your position or point of view. It is the statement that tells the reader what the entire paper is about and what you are trying to prove. The thesis statement must be included in your introductory paragraph.

Example of a Thesis Statement about the American Revolution:

> The American colonists were justified in breaking away from Great Britain as a result of the Stamp Act, the Townshend Acts, and the Boston Massacre.

> You can see how the writer took elements from the historical context and words from the task question to form the thesis statement. Go back to the historical context and task question examples and highlight those words that were incorporated into your thesis. Also, highlight these words again in the sample thesis statement. This is good practice for what you need to do on DBQ tests.

5. **Primary source documents:** Primary source documents are pieces of writing or drawings taken from the original source. They are directly related to the theme of the DBQ and are to be used when answering the task question. A primary source document can be in the form of a political cartoon, a picture, a quote, a chart, a graph, a newspaper article, or a journal. These documents **must** be used in your essay in order to support and develop your thesis statement.

Here's an example of a primary source document from the time period of the American Revolution:

**Paul Revere's engraving of the Boston Massacre**

*Source:* HistoryCentral.com

6. **Scaffolding Questions:** Scaffolding questions are questions that are directly related to the primary source documents. Answering the scaffolding questions correctly will help you interpret the documents. Your answers to the scaffolding questions may be used in your essay in order to help you explain the documents.

Here's an example of a scaffolding question about the American Revolution document given above, Paul Revere's engraving of the Boston Massacre:

**Which group in the engraving is demonstrating an abuse of power?**

The answer to this scaffolding question—the British soldiers—can be used in the actual DBQ.

Understanding and using all six elements of the DBQ will make you a creative and successful author/historian!

# Beginning Strategies

## ▶ READING FOR INFORMATION AND UNDERSTANDING

**Do you always tell the *whole* truth?**
Of course you are honest, but do you always tell every fact, every thought, every action, in your e-mail to a friend? A writer who writes about the past does the same thing you do when you don't tell all. Just like you, the writer decides what pieces of historical evidence to include and what to leave out. This makes a person reading history more like a detective trying to uncover what really happened. You need to be a strong reader in order to uncover the writer's bias toward the subject. Is the evidence correct? Is it complete? Has anything been left out? Do you agree with the writer's conclusions? This chapter is designed to give you reading strategies that will help you understand documents.

**What reading approach should I use?**
Document-based questions contain many reading selections. This means you need to be a good reader because you will be asked to quickly read many documents and *read with understanding*. The approach to reading the material in a DBQ is different from the approach used in reading a novel or other literary works. Rather than starting at the beginning and going to the end, you need to **preview** the document. (Preview means to

look at the document before reading it.) This is especially necessary when the document is different or un-familiar to you.

**How should I preview a document?**

When you preview a document, look it over quickly—reading titles, subheadings, or the first sentence of para-graphs. This is done in order to get a sense of what will be presented in the reading. Once you have previewed the document, you should have a good idea of what it is about.

**How should I read a document?**

What is the order that the documents appear? Usually, documents are arranged in **chronological order**. That means they appear in time-order from first to last. This suggests that your essay should have a chronologi-cal development.

Sometimes the documents are grouped around a point of view. This indicates that the development of your essay should be a **comparison/contrast**.

Interact with the document as you read. Stop after a topic sentence or paragraph and ask yourself: "**What is the main topic?**" "**What are the main points I just read?**" Write down these main points. Each writer has a bias about a subject. (Remember that *bias* means a writer's or reader's viewpoint. A writer could be **neu-tral**, **in favor of a subject**, or **against it**.) Write the viewpoint. Is the evidence that the writer gives correct? Is it complete? What might have been left out?

By writing down the title, topic, and writer's viewpoint, you are actually developing an introductory paragraph to your essay. An effective document-based essay introduction should answer two questions:

What is the topic?
What is the author's opinion on the topic?

If you want to write an excellent introduction, you must think of a general, attention-getting comment (hook) about the topic. If you were answering a DBQ on the Civil Rights Era, an appropriate hook might be this: **When Rosa Parks sat down, the whole world stood up.** As you complete your reading of each of the following documents, try to think of an attention-getting hook.

Practice the methods mentioned of previewing and reading, using the following documents. Be sure to read the selection quickly. Write the type of document it is, its title, and topic. Go back and read the selec-tion. Identify the writer and the time period. List the main points, writer's viewpoint, document purpose, key words and phrases that will help you understand the document, evidence that the writer's view is cor-rect, list any details that you think are not included by the writer, and state whether or not you agree or dis-agree with the writer's viewpoint. Use the following worksheets as a guide to answer DBQs.

| Preview Questions | Answers to Preview Questions |
|---|---|
| What type of document is this? | |
| What is the title of the document? | |
| What is the topic of the document? | |

STRATEGIES FOR READING THE DOCUMENT ▶

| Reading Strategy Questions | Answers to Reading Strategy Questions |
|---|---|
| Who is the writer? | |
| What is the time period? | |
| What are the main points of the document? | |
| What is the writer's viewpoint? | |

| Reading Strategy Questions | Answers to Reading Strategy Questions |
|---|---|
| What is the purpose of the document? | |
| What key words or phrases will help you understand the document? | |
| Is the evidence for the writer's viewpoint of the topic correct? | |
| Do you think the writer has omitted any important topic information, and if so, what? | |
| Do you agree or disagree with the writer's viewpoint? | |

Before you begin a document-based essay, you must spend at least five minutes reading and understanding the question. All of the documents must be previewed with the task question always in mind.

The following is a typical task question around which a DBQ would be created and supporting documents drawn.

> **Write an essay in which you discuss the ways in which the U.S. Constitution safeguards or protects the rights of American citizens.**

Now you will read documents related to this task and review strategies for previewing and reading each document.

Quickly look at the type, title, and topic of the following document.

## DOCUMENT 1

## *The Preamble*

We the people of the United States, in order to form a more perfect Union, **establish justice**, insure **domestic tranquility**, provide for the common defense, promote the general **welfare**, and secure the blessings of **liberty** to ourselves and our **posterity**, do **ordain** and establish this Constitution for the United States of America.

**establish:** set up

**domestic tranquility:** peace in one's country

**welfare:** well-being

**liberty:** freedom

**posterity:** future generations

Sample Hook:

The American citizens, in order to form a stronger country, set up a government that provides justice and freedom, protects from foreign enemies, and defends and provides a safe environment for its people and future generations by writing this Constitution.

Now, preview and read the selection. Fill in the preview and reading charts below.

PREVIEW CHART FOR DOCUMENT 1 ▶

| Preview Questions | Answers to Preview Questions |
|---|---|
| What type of document is this? | |
| What is the title of the document? | |
| What is the topic of the document? | |

| Reading Strategy Questions | Answers to Reading Strategy Questions |
|---|---|
| Who is the writer? | |
| What is the time period? | |
| What are the main points of the document? | |
| What is the writer's viewpoint? | |
| What is the purpose of the document? | |
| What key words or phrases will help you understand the document? | |
| Is the evidence for the writer's viewpoint of the topic correct? | |
| Do you think the writer has omitted any important topic information, and if so, what? | |
| Do you agree or disagree with the writer's viewpoint? | |

With the information you have, write a hook to begin your essay:

_____

_____

_____

_____

_____

_____

_____

_____

_____

_____

Compare your chart with the model charts on the following pages.

| Preview Questions | Answers to Preview Questions |
|---|---|
| What type of document is this? | This document is the introductory paragraph to the U.S. Constitution. |
| What is the title of the document? | The title of the document is the *Preamble to the Constitution.* |
| What is the topic of the document? | The topic of the document is an explanation of the purpose of the U.S. Constitution. |

STRATEGIES CHART FOR READING DOCUMENT 1 ▶

| Reading Strategy Questions | Answers to Reading Strategy Questions |
|---|---|
| Who is the writer? | The writers are the framers of the Constitution. |
| What is the time period? | The time period is 1787, when every government in Europe was a monarchy. |
| What are the main points of the document? | The main points of the document are:<br>a. "We the people" expresses the principle of popular sovereignty. This principle means that the people hold the final authority in government.<br>b. The people give the government the powers it needs to achieve its goals.<br>c. The American people expect their government to defend justice and liberty.<br>d. They expect the government to provide peace and safety from foreign enemies. |

| Reading Strategy Questions | Answers to Reading Strategy Questions |
|---|---|
| | e. The American people hold the government responsible for providing the above goals for themselves and for future generations of Americans. |
| What is the writer's viewpoint? | The writer supports one of the main principles of the Constitution, the principle of popular sovereignty. This means that the government gets its power from the people and can only govern with their consent. |
| What is the purpose of the document? | The purpose of the document is to introduce the concept of popular sovereignty. |
| What key words or phrases will help you understand the document? | We the people, justice, domestic tranquility, defense, liberty, posterity |
| Is the evidence for the writer's viewpoint of the topic correct? | Yes, the writer's evidence is correct. |
| Do you think the writer has omitted any important topic information, and if so, what? | The writer has not omitted any important topic information. |
| Do you agree or disagree with the writer's viewpoint? | I agree with the views the framers of the Constitution included in the Preamble. It is important that our government receives its power from the people. |

With the information you have, write a hook to begin your essay:

In the beginning, God created heaven and earth; in the beginning of our newly founded nation, god-fearing men created the U.S. Constitution.

Take another look at the task question below. This time you are going to read a table related to this question.

**Write an essay in which you discuss the ways in which the U.S. Constitution safeguards or protects the rights of American citizens.**

# ▶ INTERPRETING A CHART, GRAPH, OR TABLE

Sometimes the document is a chart, graph, or table. In this case you need to read the document differently. What is the title of the chart? What are the headings of the columns (top of chart) or rows (side)? What information is given? In what way can you use the information in the chart or graph to help you answer the task question? Look at the table below. Quickly find its title. Look at the rows and information.

## DOCUMENT 2

## *U.S. Constitution Ratification Table*

| State | Date | Vote |
|---|---|---|
| Connecticut | January 9, 1788 | 128–40 |
| Delaware | December 7, 1787 | 30–0 |
| Georgia | January 2, 1788 | 26–0 |
| Maryland | April 28, 1788 | 63–11 |
| Massachusetts | February 6, 1788 | 187–168 |
| New Hampshire | June 21, 1788 | 57–46 |
| New Jersey | December 19, 1787 | 38–0 |
| New York | July 26, 1788 | 30–27 |
| North Carolina | November 21, 1789 | 184–77 |
| Pennsylvania | December 12, 1787 | 30–0 |
| Rhode Island | May 29, 1790 | 34–32 |
| South Carolina | May 23, 1788 | 149–73 |
| Virginia | June 25, 1788 | 89–79 |

Now preview and read the selection. Fill in the following preview and reading charts.

| Preview Questions | Answers to Preview Questions |
|---|---|
| What type of document is this? | |
| What is the title of the document? | |
| What are the table headings? | |

STRATEGIES CHART FOR READING DOCUMENT 2 ▶

| Reading Strategy Questions | Answers to Reading Strategy Questions |
|---|---|
| What is the time period? | |
| What are the main points of the document? | |
| What is the purpose of the document? | |
| What are the key words and phrases that will help me understand the document? | |

Compare your answers to the following model charts.

| Preview Questions | Answers to Preview Questions |
| --- | --- |
| What type of document is this? | This document is a table showing the years, votes, and states that ratified the Constitution. |
| What is the title? | The title of this document is "U.S. Constitution Ratification Table." |
| What are the headings? | The headings are the states, years of ratification, and the votes. |

STRATEGIES CHART FOR READING DOCUMENT 2 ▶

| Reading Strategy Questions | Answers to Reading Strategy Questions |
| --- | --- |
| What is the time period? | The time period is from 1787–1790. |
| What are the main points of the document? | The main points of the document are:<br>a. All thirteen states ratified the Constitution. This showed the unity of the individual states in supporting a strong, central government.<br>b. Massachusetts, New York, and Virginia's votes were close. |
| What is the purpose of the document? | The purpose of the document is to show how many states ratified the Constitution, the years of ratification, and how close the votes were. |
| What key words or phrases will help you understand the document? | The key word that will help me to understand the document is "ratification." |

## *Article V*

The **Congress**, whenever two-thirds of both houses shall **deem** it necessary, shall propose **amendments** to this Constitution, or, on the application of the **legislatures** of two-thirds of the several states, shall call a **convention** for proposing amendments, which, in either case, shall be valid to all intents and purposes, as part of this Constitution, when **ratified** by the legislatures of three-fourths of the several states, or by conventions in three-fourths thereof, as the one or the other mode of ratification may be proposed by the Congress; provided that no amendments which may be made **prior** to the year 1808 shall in any manner affect the first and fourth clauses in the Ninth Section of the First Article; and that no state, without its **consent** shall be **deprived** of its equal **suffrage** in the **Senate.**

---

**Congress:** the legislative branch of government made up of two houses: the Senate and the House of Representatives. Together, the two houses have the power to make laws that govern all fifty states.

**deem:** to consider, to judge

**amendments:** formal, written changes

**legislature:** branch of government that passes laws

**convention:** a meeting of delegates from each state

**ratified:** approved

**prior:** beforehand

**consent:** permission

**deprived:** taken away

**Senate:** smaller house of Congress, in which each state has two senators as representatives

**suffrage:** right to vote

---

Now, fill in the following preview and reading charts.

| Preview Questions | Answers to Preview Questions |
|---|---|
| What type of document is this? | |
| What is the title of the document? | |
| What is the topic of the document? | |

STRATEGIES CHART FOR READING DOCUMENT 3 ▶

| Reading Strategy Questions | Answers to Reading Strategy Questions |
|---|---|
| Who is the writer? | |
| What is the time period? | |
| What are the main points of the document? | |
| What is the writer's viewpoint? | |

| Reading Strategy Questions | Answers to Reading Strategy Questions |
|---|---|
| What is the purpose of the document? | |
| What key words or phrases will help you understand the document? | |
| Is the evidence for the writer's viewpoint of the topic correct? | |
| Do you think the writer has omitted any important topic information, and if so, what? | |
| Do you agree or disagree with the writer's viewpoint? | |

With the information you have, write a hook to begin your essay:

_____

_____

_____

_____

_____

_____

_____

_____

Compare your answers to the following model charts.

| Preview Questions | Answers to Preview Questions |
|---|---|
| What type of document is this? | This document is the fifth of seven Articles that explain the Constitution. |
| What is the title of the document? | The title of the document is Article V. |
| What is the topic of the document? | The topic of Article V is the provisions for amendment to the Constitution. |

| Reading Strategy Questions | Answers to Reading Strategy Questions |
|---|---|
| Who is the writer? | The writers are the framers of the Constitution. |
| What is the time period? | The time period is 1787. |
| What are the main points of the document? | The main points of the document are these:<br>a. The Constitution can be amended, or changed, if necessary.<br>b. An amendment can be proposed in two ways:<br>(1) a two-thirds vote of both houses of Congress |

| Reading Strategy Questions | Answers to Reading Strategy Questions |
|---|---|
| | (2) a national convention called by Congress at the request of two-thirds of the state legislatures (This second method has never been used.)<br>c. An amendment must be ratified, or approved, by<br>(1) three-fourths of the state legislatures or<br>(2) special conventions in three-fourths of the states (Congress decides which method will be used.) |
| What is the writer's viewpoint? | The framers of the Constitution could not predict all possible future problems. |
| What is the purpose of the document? | They wanted to ensure that the Constitution would be a useful and flexible document for all generations of Americans to come. Therefore, they created a mechanism for changing it when necessary. |
| What key words or phrases will help you understand the document? | The key words that will help me to understand the document are these:<br>a. Congress<br>b. Legislature<br>c. convention<br>d. ratified<br>e. prior<br>f. consent<br>g. deprived<br>h. suffrage |
| Is the evidence for the writer's viewpoint of the topic correct? | Yes, the writer's evidence is correct. |
| Do you think the writer has omitted any important topic information, and if so, what? | No, the writer has not omitted any information. |

| Reading Strategy Questions | Answers to Reading Strategy Questions |
| --- | --- |
| Do you agree or disagree with the writer's viewpoint? | I agree with the writer's viewpoint. A document's flexibility is its strength. Thus far, our Constitution has stood the test of time because of the framers' wise inclusion of a procedure for change. This mechanism has allowed for 27 amendments to be added to the Constitution since its ratification in 1790. |

With the information you have, write a hook to begin your essay:

Long after buildings have been cleared and people have passed on, the written word shall remain.

## DOCUMENT 4

## *Amendment 1*

Congress shall make no law respecting an establishment of religion, or **prohibiting** the free exercise thereof; or **abridging** the freedom of speech, or of the press; or the right of the people peaceably to **assemble**, and to **petition** the government for a **redress** of **grievances.**

> **prohibiting:** stopping
>
> **abridging:** limiting
>
> **assemble:** gather
>
> **petition:** ask
>
> **redress:** correct
>
> **grievances:** wrongs

Now, try to complete the following preview and strategies for reading charts for Document 4.

| Preview Questions | Answers to Preview Questions |
|---|---|
| What type of document is this? | |
| What is the title of the document? | |
| What is the topic of the document? | |

STRATEGIES CHART FOR READING DOCUMENT 4 ▶

| Reading Strategy Questions | Answers to Reading Strategy Questions |
|---|---|
| Who is the writer? | |
| What is the time period? | |
| What are the main points of the document? | |
| What is the writer's viewpoint? | |

| Reading Strategy Questions | Answers to Reading Strategy Questions |
|---|---|
| What is the purpose of the document? | |
| What key words or phrases will help you understand the document? | |
| Is the evidence for the writer's viewpoint of the topic correct? | |
| Do you think the writer has omitted any important topic information, and if so, what? | |
| Do you agree or disagree with the writer's viewpoint? | |

With the information you have, write a hook to begin your essay:

_____

_____

_____

_____

_____

_____

_____

_____

_____

Compare your answers to the following model charts.

PREVIEW CHART FOR DOCUMENT 4 ▶

| Preview Questions | Answers to Preview Questions |
| --- | --- |
| What type of document is this? | This document is an excerpt of the Bill of Rights that is contained in the U.S. Constitution. |
| What is the title of the document? | The title of this document is the First Amendment. |
| What is the topic of the document? | The topic of the document is the protection of basic rights: freedom of religion, speech, press, assembly, and petition. |

STRATEGIES CHART FOR READING DOCUMENT 4 ▶

| Reading Strategy Questions | Answers to Reading Strategy Questions |
| --- | --- |
| Who is the writer? | The writers are the framers of the Constitution. |
| What is the time period? | The time period is 1791, the year in which the Bill of Rights was added to the U.S. Constitution. |
| What are the main points of the document? | The main points of the document are:<br>a. Congress cannot set up an official church or religion for the country.<br>b. Congress protects freedom of speech.<br>c. The government must ensure freedom of the press. |

| Reading Strategy Questions | Answers to Reading Strategy Questions |
| --- | --- |
| | d. The government must allow people to assemble.<br><br>e. The government must give people the right to petition the government for a redress of grievances. |
| What is the writer's viewpoint? | The framers of the Constitution believed that government should not be allowed to favor one religion over another. In colonial times, colonies had established churches. This led to the persecution of the minority. They also believed that all citizens have a right to free speech, as well as no censorship of books or newspapers. In addition, they supported people's right to peacefully hold public meetings. The writers strongly felt that individuals should have an established procedure for asking the government to correct wrongdoings. |
| What is the purpose of the document? | The purpose of this document is to specifically discuss the five basic rights of freedom of religion, speech, the press, assembly, and petition. |
| What key words or phrases will help you understand the document? | The key words that will help me to understand the document are:<br>1. prohibiting<br>2. abridging<br>3. assemble<br>4. petition<br>5. redress<br>6. grievances |
| Is the evidence for the writer's viewpoint of the topic correct? | Yes, the writer's evidence is correct. |
| Do you think the writer has omitted any important topic information, and if so, what? | No, the writer has not omitted any information. |

| Reading Strategy Questions | Answers to Reading Strategy Questions |
|---|---|
| Do you agree or disagree with the writer's viewpoint? | I agree with the writers of the document. It is essential that individuals have the basic right to worship, speak, and write freely; to read books, newspapers, and see movies without censorship; to meet peacefully; and to ask the government to correct wrongdoings. |

With the information you have, write a hook to begin your essay:

The First Amendment has had a profound impact on the lives of Oprah Winfrey, Martin Luther King, Jr., N'Sync, Larry King, and Madonna. If it were not for this amendment, the messages and ideas of these insightful people would be plagued with a deafening silence.

## DOCUMENT 5

### *Amendment 15, Section One*

The right of citizens of the United States to vote shall not be **denied** or **abridged** by the United States or any state on the account of **race**, color, or **previous** condition of **servitude.**

> **denied:** withheld
>
> **abridged:** limited
>
> **race:** ethnic group
>
> **previous:** earlier
>
> **servitude:** slavery

Now, try to complete the following preview and strategies for reading charts for Document 5.

| Preview Questions | Answers to Preview Questions |
| --- | --- |
| What type of document is this? | |
| What is the title of the document? | |
| What is the topic of the document? | |
| Who is the writer? | |
| What is the time period? | |
| What are the main points of the document? | |
| What is the writer's viewpoint? | |
| What is the purpose of the document? | |
| What key words or phrases will help you understand the document? | |

| Reading Strategy Questions | Answers to Reading Strategy Questions |
|---|---|
| Is the evidence for the writer's viewpoint of the topic correct? | |
| Do you think the writer has omitted any important topic information, and if so, what? | |
| Do you agree or disagree with the writer's viewpoint? | |

With the information you have, write a hook to begin your essay:

_____

_____

_____

_____

_____

_____

_____

_____

_____

Compare your answers to following the model charts.

| Preview Questions | Answers to Preview Questions |
|---|---|
| What type of document is this? | This document is an excerpt of the Bill of Rights that is contained in the U.S. Constitution. |
| What is the title of the document? | The title of the document is the Fifteenth Amendment, Section One. |
| What is the topic of the document? | The document's topic is protecting the voting rights of individuals. |
| Who is the writer? | The writers are the framers of the Constitution. |
| What is the time period? | The time period is 1870. Prior to that year, most African Americans, women, and Native Americans were either discouraged or prohibited from voting. |
| What are the main points of the document? | The main points of the document are:<br>a. No person can be denied the right to vote because of race, color, or former slave status.<br>b. This amendment gave African Americans the right to vote. |
| What is the writer's viewpoint? | The writers believed that African Americans should be able to vote. In the 1800s southern states used poll taxes, literacy tests, and grandfather clauses to keep African Americans from voting. |
| What is the purpose of the document? | The purpose of the document is to explain that voting rights were extended to African Americans. |

| Reading Strategy Questions | Answers to Reading Strategy Questions |
|---|---|
| What key words or phrases will help you understand the document? | The key words or phrases that will help me understand the document are:<br>a. denied<br>b. race<br>c. previous<br>d. servitude |
| Is the evidence for the writer's viewpoint of the topic correct? | Yes, the writers' evidence is correct. |
| Do you think the writer has omitted any important topic information, and if so, what? | No, the writers have not omitted any information. |
| Do you agree or disagree with the writer's viewpoint? | I agree with the writers' views that the powerful right to vote must be protected and should not be withheld from any citizen. |

With the information you have, write a hook to begin your essay:

One major difference between our democratic society and dictatorships is the powerful right of each United States citizen to vote.

## DOCUMENT 6

## *Amendment 19*

The right of citizens of the United States to vote shall not be **denied** or **abridged** by the United States or by any state on the account of sex.

Now, try to complete the following preview and strategies for reading charts for Document 6.

| Preview Questions | Answers to Preview Questions |
|---|---|
| What type of document is this? | |
| What is the title of the document? | |
| What is the topic of the document? | |

STRATEGIES CHART FOR READING DOCUMENT 6 ▶

| Reading Strategy Questions | Answers to Reading Strategy Questions |
|---|---|
| Who is the writer? | |
| What is the time period? | |
| What are the main points of the document? | |
| What is the writer's viewpoint? | |

| Reading Strategy Questions | Answers to Reading Strategy Questions |
| --- | --- |
| What is the purpose of the document? | |
| What key words or phrases will help you understand the document? | |
| Is the evidence for the writer's viewpoint of the topic correct? | |
| Do you think the writer has omitted any important topic information, and if so, what? | |
| Do you agree or disagree with the writer's viewpoint? | |

With the information you have, write a hook to begin your essay:

_____

_____

_____

_____

_____

_____

_____

Compare your answers to the following model charts.

| Preview Questions | Answers to Preview Questions |
| --- | --- |
| What type of document is this? | This document is one of the 27 amendments to the U.S. Constitution. |
| What is the title of the document? | The title of the document is the Nineteenth Amendment. |
| What is the topic of the document? | The topic of the document is protecting the voting rights of women. |

| Reading Strategy Questions | Answers to Reading Strategy Questions |
| --- | --- |
| Who is the writer? | The writers are the framers of the Constitution. |
| What is the time period? | The time period is 1920, the year that women received the right to vote. |
| What are the main points of the document? | The main point of the document is that no person can be denied the right to vote on account of his or her sex. |
| What is the writer's viewpoint? | The writers believed that all citizens, no matter what their sex, have the right to vote. |

| Reading Strategy Questions | Answers to Reading Strategy Questions |
|---|---|
| What is the purpose of the document? | The purpose of the document is specifically to discuss the right to vote. |
| What key words or phrases will help you understand the document? | The key words or phrases that will help me understand the document are the following:<br>a. denied<br>b. abridged<br>c. suffrage |
| Is the evidence for the writer's viewpoint of the topic correct? | Yes, the writer's evidence is correct. |
| Do you think the writer has omitted any important topic information, and if so, what? | No, the writer has not omitted any information. |
| Do you agree or disagree with the writer's viewpoint? | I agree with the writers' viewpoint that eligible voters must have their voting rights protected no matter what their sex. This amendment to the Constitution helped set the foundation for gender equality. |

With the information you have, write a hook to begin your essay:

In the 1920 Presidential election, a single vote catapulted the women's movement into a new era of history. Charlotte Woodward, an activist for women's rights who attended the Seneca Falls Convention, used her hard-won right to cast her vote for the next President of the United States.

# DOCUMENT 7

## *Amendment 4*

The right of the people to be **secure** in their persons, houses, papers, and **effects**, against unreasonable searches and **seizures**, shall not be **violated**; and no **warrants** shall issue but upon probable cause, supported by **oath** or **affirmation**, and particularly describing the place to be searched, and the persons or things to be seized.

**secure:** safe

**effects:** belongings

**seizures:** taking away

**violated:** ignored

**warrants:** written court orders

**oath:** promise

**affirmation:** proof

Now, try to complete the following preview and strategies for the reading charts for Document 7.

**PREVIEW CHART FOR DOCUMENT 7** ▶

| Preview Questions | Answers to Preview Questions |
|---|---|
| What type of document is this? | |
| What is the title of the document? | |
| What is the topic of the document? | |

| Reading Strategy Questions | Answers to Reading Strategy Questions |
| --- | --- |
| Who is the writer? | |
| What is the time period? | |
| What are the main points of the document? | |
| What is the writer's viewpoint? | |
| What is the purpose of the document? | |
| What key words or phrases will help you understand the document? | |
| Is the evidence for the writer's viewpoint of the topic correct? | |
| Do you think the writer has omitted any important topic information, and if so, what? | |
| Do you agree or disagree with the writer's viewpoint? | |

With the information you have, write a hook to begin your essay:

_____

_____

_____

_____

_____

_____

_____

_____

_____

_____

Compare your answers with the following model charts.

**PREVIEW CHART FOR DOCUMENT 7** ▶

| Preview Questions | Answers to Preview Questions |
| --- | --- |
| What type of document is this? | This document is an excerpt of the Bill of Rights that is contained in the U.S. Constitution. |
| What is the title of the document? | The title of the document is Amendment 4. |
| What is the topic of the document? | The document's topic is about protecting the rights of the individual against unlawful search and seizure. |

| Reading Strategy Questions | Answers to Reading Strategy Questions |
| --- | --- |
| Who is the writer? | The writers are the framers of the Constitution. |
| What is the time period? | The time period is 1791, the year in which the Bill of Rights was added to the U.S. Constitution. |
| What are the main points of the document? | The main points of the document are:<br>a. No citizen can have an unreasonable search and seizure.<br>b. Search and seizures are allowed only if a judge has issued a warrant, or written court order.<br>c. A warrant is issued only if there is probable cause, that it is likely that the search will show evidence of a crime.<br>d. A search warrant must name the exact place to be searched and things to be seized. |
| What is the writer's viewpoint? | The framers of the Constitution believed that unless it can be shown that a person is likely to be involved in a crime, it is violating that person's rights to search and seize the individual's possessions. |
| What is the purpose of the document? | The purpose of the document is to discuss citizens' rights against unreasonable search and seizure. |
| What key words or phrases will help you understand the document? | The key words or phrases that will help me understand the document are:<br>a. secure<br>b. effects<br>c. unreasonable<br>d. seizures<br>e. violated<br>f. warrants<br>g. oath<br>h. affirmation |

| Reading Strategy Questions | Answers to Reading Strategy Questions |
|---|---|
| Is the evidence for the writer's viewpoint of the topic correct? | Yes, the writer's evidence is correct. |
| Do you think the writer has omitted any important topic information, and if so, what? | No, the writer has not omitted any information. |
| Do you agree or disagree with the writer's viewpoint? | I agree with the views of the framers of the Constitution included in Amendment 4. I would not want the government to be able to search my home and property without just cause. It is important that individuals are protected from unnecessary government intrusion into their everyday lives. |

With the information you have, write a hook to begin your essay:

How would you and your family feel if military personnel entered your home without your invitation, searched your house, and left with your possessions?

## DOCUMENT 8

## *Amendment 5*

No person shall be held to answer for a **capital,** or otherwise **infamous** crime, unless on a presentment or **indictment** of a grand jury, except in cases arising in the land or naval forces, or in the militia, when in actual service in time of war or public danger; nor shall any person be subject for the same offense to be twice put in **jeopardy** of life and limb; nor shall be **compelled**, in any criminal case, to be a witness against himself; nor be **deprived** of life, liberty, or property, without **due process** of law; nor shall private property be taken for public use, without just **compensation.**

**capital crime:** a crime punishable by death

**infamous:** notoriously bad

**indictment:** accusation

**jeopardy:** danger

**compelled:** forced

**deprived:** denied

**due process:** fair trial

**compensation:** payment

Now that you have had some practice, try to complete the following preview and strategies charts for reading Document 8.

PREVIEW CHART FOR DOCUMENT 8 ▶

| Preview Questions | Answers to Preview Questions |
|---|---|
| What type of document is this? | |
| What is the title of the document? | |
| What is the topic of the document? | |

| Reading Strategy Questions | Answers to Reading Strategy Questions |
|---|---|
| Who is the writer? | |
| What is the time period? | |
| What are the main points of the document? | |
| What is the writer's viewpoint? | |

| Reading Strategy Questions | Answers to Reading Strategy Questions |
|---|---|
| What is the purpose of the document? | |
| What key words or phrases will help you understand the document? | |
| Is the evidence for the writer's viewpoint of the topic correct? | |
| Do you think the writer has omitted any important topic information, and if so, what? | |
| Do you agree or disagree with the writer's viewpoint? | |

With the information you have, write a hook to begin your essay:

_____

_____

_____

_____

_____

_____

_____

_____

_____

Compare your answers to the following model charts.

PREVIEW CHART FOR DOCUMENT 8 ▶

| Preview Questions | Answers to Preview Questions |
| --- | --- |
| What type of document is this? | This document is an excerpt of the Bill of Rights that is contained in the U.S. Constitution. |
| What is the title of the document? | The title of the document is the Amendment 5. |
| What is the topic of the document? | The document's topic is protecting the rights of someone who is accused of a crime. |

| Reading Strategy Questions | Answers to Reading Strategy Questions |
| --- | --- |
| Who is the writer? | The writers are the framers of the Constitution. |
| What is the time period? | The time period is 1791, the year in which the Bill of Rights was added to the U.S. Constitution. |
| What are the main points of the document? | The main points of the document are:<br>a. No person can be accused of a crime unless they are indicted (formally accused) by a grand jury.<br>b. You cannot be tried for the same crime twice.<br>c. You cannot be forced to testify against yourself or give information that would be self-incriminating.<br>d. You have the right to a fair trial.<br>e. The government cannot take away your property without paying you an adequate price for it. |
| What is the writer's viewpoint? | The framers of the Constitution believed that those who were accused of a crime were entitled to certain rights that the government could not take away. |
| What is the purpose of the document? | The purpose of the document is to specifically discuss the rights to which those accused of a crime are entitled. |
| What key words or phrases will help you understand the document? | The key words that will help me to understand the document are:<br>a. indictment<br>b. grand jury<br>c. jeopardy<br>d. deprived<br>e. compensation |

| Is the evidence for the writer's viewpoint of the topic correct? | Yes, the writer's evidence is correct. |
| Do you think the writer has omitted any important topic information, and if so, what? | The writer has not omitted any important topic information. |
| Do you agree or disagree with the writer's viewpoint? | I agree with the views the framers of the Constitution included in the Fifth Amendment. It is important, that as American citizens, we are entitled to certain rights when we are accused of a crime. Without it, we could be imprisoned for years without a trial. |

With the information you have, write a hook to begin your essay:

There are countries today that can arrest citizens and literally throw away the key, leaving them to perish in jail.

# DOCUMENT 9

## *Amendment 10*

The powers not **delegated** to the United States by the Constitution, nor **prohibited** by it to the states, are **reserved** to the states respectively, or to the people.

---

**delegated:** given out

**prohibited:** stopped

**reserved:** set aside

---

Now, you can go on to complete the following preview and strategies for reading charts for Document 9.

| Preview Questions | Answers to Preview Questions |
|---|---|
| What type of document is this? | |
| What is the title of the document? | |
| What is the topic of the document? | |

STRATEGIES CHART FOR READING DOCUMENT 9 ▶

| Reading Strategy Questions | Answers to Reading Strategy Questions |
|---|---|
| Who is the writer? | |
| What is the time period? | |
| What are the main points of the document? | |
| What is the writer's viewpoint? | |

| Reading Strategy Questions | Answers to Reading Strategy Questions |
|---|---|
| What is the purpose of the document? | |
| What key words or phrases will help you understand the document? | |
| Is the evidence for the writer's viewpoint of the topic correct? | |
| Do you think the writer has omitted any important topic information, and if so, what? | |
| Do you agree or disagree with the writer's viewpoint? | |

With the information you have, write a hook to begin your essay:

_____

_____

_____

_____

_____

_____

_____

_____

Compare your answers to the following model charts.

| Preview Questions | Answers to Preview Questions |
| --- | --- |
| What type of document is this? | This document is an excerpt of the Bill of Rights that is contained in the U.S. Constitution. |
| What is the title of the document? | The title of the document is Amendment 10. |
| What is the topic of the document? | The document's topic is limiting the power of the federal government. |

STRATEGIES CHART FOR READING DOCUMENT 9 ▶

| Reading Strategy Questions | Answers to Reading Strategy Questions |
| --- | --- |
| Who is the writer? | The writers are the framers of the Constitution. |
| What is the time period? | The time period is 1791, the year in which the Bill of Rights was added to the U.S. Constitution. |
| What are the main points of the document? | The main points of the document are:<br>a. This amendment limits the power of the federal government.<br>b. Powers not given to the federal government belong to the states.<br>c. The powers reserved to the states are not listed in the U.S. Constitution. |
| What is the writer's viewpoint? | The writer's viewpoint is that the power of the national government should be limited. |

| Reading Strategy Questions | Answers to Reading Strategy Questions |
|---|---|
| What is the purpose of the document? | The purpose of the document is to limit the power of the federal government. Any power not given specifically to the federal government by the constitution is reserved, or set aside, for the states. |
| What key words or phrases will help you understand the document? | Key words or phrases that will help me understand the document are: <br> a. delegated <br> b. prohibited <br> c. reserved |
| Is the evidence for the writer's viewpoint of the topic correct? | Yes, the evidence for the writer's viewpoint of the topic is correct. |
| Do you think the writer has omitted any important topic information, and if so, what? | The writer has not omitted any important topic information. |

With the information you have, write a hook to begin your essay:

How were the Founding Fathers able to invest power in a particular body of government, while safeguarding American citizens against tyranny?

## ▶ HIGH FREQUENCY WORDS

Did you ever feel left out because you didn't understand the special language of a particular group? You are not alone. Many students get that left out feeling when they see certain words that appear in directions and on tests. This section will introduce many of the words that appear quite often in essay directions and on tests, especially DBQ tests. They will be defined for you and used in direction examples. Try to become familiar with as many of these words as possible. This will help you read and understand the document-based questions better. It will also help you improve your essay writing. Try to use these words in your writing.

| High Frequency Words | Definitions | Examples and usage in text |
|---|---|---|
| **advantages** and **disadvantages** | An advantage is a benefit, a help. On the other hand, a disadvantage is the opposite of an advantage. It is a difficulty or setback. | These two words usually appear together in essay directions.<br>• What were the **advantages** and **disadvantages** of having a Constitution?<br>• What were the **advantages** and **disadvantages** of keeping the states strong? |
| **affect/effect** | Affect means to influence or change (not to be confused with *effect,* which means result). | • How did the ability to amend the Constitution **affect** its value?<br>• What **effect** did the Anti-Federalists have over the votes for ratification of the Constitution? |
| **analyze** | To analyze is to examine, look at closely. | • **Analyze** the time line of the ratification of the Constitution:<br>    **1787**<br>    The Constitutional Convention begins.<br>    **1788**<br>    The required amount of states ratify the Constitution.<br>    **1789**<br>    The Constitution is sent to the states for approval.<br>    **1789**<br>    The Bill of Rights is proposed.<br>    **1790**<br>    The final state approves the Constitution.<br>  By **analyzing** (examining) each event in the time line, you are being asked to write about the historical importance (significance) of each event. You should explain the event and its impact (influence or change) on history. |
| **based** | Based means founded upon or supported. The support or foundation that something is built upon is its base. | The stronger the foundation or **base**, the stronger the object or idea that is built on it. It is the same thing with ideas and events. The word **basis** is related to the word based and means support. |

| High Frequency Words | Definitions | Examples and usage in text |
|---|---|---|
| | | What was the **basis** of the Federalists' support for the ratification of the Constitution? The creation of Article Five of the Constitution was **based** on what reasons? |
| **cause** and **effect** | The cause is an action or reason why something happens. (The word *cause* is not the same as *because*. Don't substitute *cause* for *because*.) The effect is the result | What were the **causes** of the Revolutionary War? What was the **cause** and **effect** of making the election of the President indirect rather than direct? |
| **central issue** | The central issue is the main idea. | What was the **central issue** the Federalists and the Anti-Federalists focused on during the ratification process of the Constitution? |
| **choose** | To choose is to select. | You have a choice. You are not supposed to complete everything. This means you will be asked to select a particular number—one, two, or perhaps three. Next, you will be asked to write something about your selection. Pay attention to how many you must select and what you are supposed to do with your choice. **Choose** one political party and explain how it came to power. **Choose** one amendment from the Bill of Rights and explain its importance. |
| **chronological** | presented in time order | It is a good idea to organize your writing in **chronological order** if you can. When you read a table, chart, or graph, see if it's in chronological order. Timelines are already in chronological order. Directions: Read the table called "Ratifying the Constitution." This lists—in **chronological** order—the process of how the Constitution became ratified. |

| High Frequency Words | Definitions | Examples and usage in text |
| --- | --- | --- |
| cite | To cite something is to quote something, to name and give credit to an original source. | Be sure to **cite** the documents you use in your essay by stating titles and authors. |
| clues | Clues are hints given to help you understand the text. | Carefully examine the **clues** in the text you are reading. |
| **compare** and **contrast** | These verbs are often found together in essay directions. Compare means showing how something is similar. Contrast means showing the differences. Whenever you see these words you must be careful to give specific details of either similarities or differences. | **Compare** and **contrast** the positions of the Federalists and the Anti-Federalists. |
| conclusion | When you are asked to come to a conclusion about an action or event, you are being asked to state the result and impact (change or influence) on historical events.<br><br>When you write a conclusion, you sum up the major points of the essay. | What **conclusions** can be reached about the Puritan influence on American life in the 1700s? |
| conflict | A conflict is a problem, struggle, disagreement, or battle. | When you are asked to write about a **conflict**, you should explain what historical event is happening (the historical context). You need to describe the conflict. Explain all sides, those who support a particular view and those who oppose it. |
| connect | To connect is to show a relationship between two things, people, or ideas. | In Sojourner Truth's speech, what **connection** does she make between men and women? |
| context | It is the background, framework, or environment in which something happens. | The **historical context** of a document includes the following: economic setting, social setting, and political setting. It provides background information relating to the theme of the document-based question. This information is useful in helping you gain insight into the theme and can also be used to help you write the introduction to the essay. |

| High Frequency Words | Definitions | Examples and usage in text |
|---|---|---|
| context (continued) | | Example: After the French and Indian War, the American colonists encountered a series of events as a result of rulings handed down from the British Parliament. These proceedings included the Proclamation of 1763, Stamp Act, Sugar Act, Quartering Act, and the Boston Massacre. The American colonists believed these acts to be an infringement of their rights since they had no vote in Parliament. |
| contributions | Contributions are helping actions. | What **contributions** did Dorothea Dix make in aiding prison reform? |
| correlate | Correlate means to show a connection or relationship between things. | What was the **correlation** between slaves and women in early nineteenth century America? |
| define | To define something is to name it, describe it in detail, label it, and classify it. | Don't simply give details. Show how the thing you are defining differs from other things.<br>**Define** the Underground Railroad. |
| demonstrate | To demonstrate means to show, illustrate, clearly explain, and give ideas supporting a position. | How did supporters of the Temperance movement **demonstrate** their disapproval for the drinking of alcohol? |
| describe | To describe means to tell about something in great detail. | **Describe** how women used their traditional roles in the home to reform American society. |
| details | Details are the facts, the support information a writer needs to develop a topic, prove a point, or make a connection in the writing. | **Details** should be used in all DBQs. Use them to answer questions such as what, how, and why.<br>What were the arguments for and against tax-supported public schools? |
| determine | To determine something is to decide or come to a decision. | **Determine** how valid the southern plantation owners' argument was that northern industrialists took no personal responsibility for their workers, while planters, on the other hand, took a personal interest in the well-being of their slaves. |

| High Frequency Words | Definitions | Examples and usage in text |
| --- | --- | --- |
| diagram | A diagram is an illustration. | Create a **diagram** showing the economic differences between the northern states and the southern states during the Civil War. |
| different | If things are different, they are not the same. | Explain how **different** ethnic groups assimilated into the American culture. |
| discuss | Discuss means to carefully analyze, examine, and give reasons for or against a topic. | When you discuss a topic you must define it, write about its historical context, and give facts, examples, and details that support your point of view about the topic.  **Discuss** the Women's Suffrage Movement in the nineteenth century. |
| document | A document is anything that can be read: a map, a diary, a letter, a bill, a cartoon, a chart, or a table. | A document-based question refers to a question that is answered using the written documents on the test.  Using information from the **documents** (including quotations and references) and your knowledge of geography, write an essay in which you explain how geography influences the lives of people who settle in a particular area. |
| elaborate | To elaborate means to develop a point of view or description giving many important details, examples, and reasons of support. | **Elaborate** on the achievements of feminist leaders throughout American history. |
| evidence | Evidence is proof, a verification of facts. | What **evidence** does the writer give for his argument against slavery? |
| example | An example is a detail, illustration, or fact about a topic. | Give three **examples** of how the revolution in France divided Americans. |
| explain | To explain means to clarify, interpret, and spell out the topic you present in your essay. | **Explain** the role of newspapers in the politics of the late 1800s. |
| explore | To explore means to investigate. | **Explore** the reasons why the United States was unsuccessful in combating Communism in Vietnam. |

| High Frequency Words | Definitions | Examples and usage in text |
| --- | --- | --- |
| fact | A fact is a detail, a piece of information, or truth. | List three **facts** about the Industrial Revolution. |
| familiarize | Familiarize means to make known. | **Familiarize** yourself with the events leading to WWI. |
| graphic organizer | A graphic organizer is any visual aid, like a chart, outline, or diagram. | You would use a **graphic organizer** to put your document answers into a clear order. |
| identify | Identify means to point out and label a specific item. | **Identify** the five principles on which the U.S. Constitution is based. |
| illustrate | Illustrate means to show. | **Illustrate** the ways in which the Underground Railroad functioned. |
| influence | When you describe the influence of something you are being asked to tell about its impact on (how it changed) society, living/working conditions, events, ideas, and so on. | To discuss the **influence** of something is to describe how something has changed because of a person, event, or idea. |
| interaction | The connection or relationship between two events, people, or ideas. | Discuss the **interaction** between the Viet Cong and the American soldiers. |
| interpret | To interpret means to translate, give examples of, solve, or comment on a topic, usually giving your viewpoint about the subject. | When you are asked to **interpret** a topic in a DBQ, be sure to include the historical context.<br><br>**Interpret** Amendment Five of the U.S. Constitution. |
| introduce | When you are asked to introduce a person, event, or idea, you need to formally and clearly present all important facts and issues concerning the subject.<br><br>When you are asked to introduce a person, event, or idea, you are being asked to explain the historical context. | **Introduce** the concept of Industrialism. |
| issues | An issue is a subject, topic, matter, problem, question, or concern. | In history, there are three types of **issues**: economic, social, and political. |

| High Frequency Words | Definitions | Examples and usage in text |
|---|---|---|
| judge/justify | To judge a person or event means to form an opinion about it.<br><br>Justify means to prove or give reasons for decisions or conclusions, making sure you are convincing. | When you make a **judgment**, you need to **justify** your viewpoint. |
| list | To list is to write an itemized series of concise statements. | **List** the causes of the Civil War. |
| locate | Locate means to find something. | When completing a DBQ, you will be asked to **locate** something on a chart, table, or map. |
| observe | Observe means to examine. | **Observe** the treatment of African-Americans throughout American history. |
| opinion | An opinion is a writer's viewpoint. | In Document A, what is the cartoonist's **opinion** about slave owners? |
| organize | To organize is to clearly arrange your ideas in a certain order. | After reading the documents, **organize** your thoughts in the graphic organizer. |
| paraphrase | When you paraphrase, you restate information in your own words. | **Paraphrase** the Preamble to the Constitution. |
| point of view | The reader or writer's point of view is that person's perspective and opinion. | What is the **point of view** of the writer in Document B? |
| predict | To predict is to guess what will happen in the future. | In a document-based question, you might be asked to judge a prediction.<br><br>Why did Lincoln **predict** the Union could be saved with his Emancipation Proclamation? |
| reason | A reason is a motive, cause, or justification. | What were the **reasons** that the southern states seceded from the Union? |
| record | To record means to write facts about an event. | **Record** the causes of the American Revolution to justify the patriot position. |
| relationship | When you are asked to show the relationship between people, events, or ideas, you are being asked to show the their connection or association. | Explain the **relationship** between the buffalo and the Plains Indians. |
| represent | To represent is to symbolize, stand for, or depict. | Why was the eagle selected to **represent** the United States? |

| High Frequency Words | Definitions | Examples and usage in text |
|---|---|---|
| research | Research is a systematic investigation in order to establish facts and reach new conclusions. | **Research** the importance of women in Native American nations. |
| resolution | A resolution is an answer or solution. | Explain the Gulf of Tonkin **Resolution**. |
| respond | Respond means to answer. | **Respond** to the "I Have a Dream" speech delivered by Martin Luther King, Jr. |
| restate | Restate means to put in your own words, to paraphrase. | **Restate** Chief Joseph Seattle's speech about the environment. |
| rubric | A rubric is an explanation of how your writing will be graded. | Use the writing **rubric** to help you revise and edit your essay. |
| select | Select means to choose. | Why do you think Emma Lazarus's poem, "The New Colossus" was **selected** to be carved at the base of the Statue of Liberty? |
| sequence | A sequence is a chronological, time order listing. | List the **sequence** of events that led to the Revolutionary War. |
| similar | When you are asked to show how things are similar, you find characteristics that they have in common. | How were Harriet Tubman and Moses **similar?** |
| suggest | To suggest is to bring to mind. To suggest also means to propose, as in a plan or theory. | The political cartoon **suggests** that in New York City, Boss William Tweed acted as a vulture destroying the city. |
| support | To support an idea in writing is to give reinforcement and back up details. | Progressives were forward-thinking people of the late nineteenth and early twentieth centuries who **supported** improvements in American life. |
| symbol | A symbol is a representation or depiction of an idea. | The Statue of Liberty is a **symbol** of freedom. |

| High Frequency Words | Definitions | Examples and usage in text |
|---|---|---|
| thesis | A thesis statement is a statement that allows the reader to understand your point of view. It is the statement that tells the reader what the paper is about and what point you are trying to prove. The thesis statement must be included in your introduction. | The following is an example of a **thesis** statement: The American colonists were justified in breaking away from Great Britain as a result of the Stamp Act, the Townshend Acts, and the Boston Massacre. |
| topic | The topic is your subject matter. | The **topic** of the document-based question is "How does geography affect culture?" |
| visualize | To visualize is to imagine. | **Visualize** what life was like for the Confederate soldier. |

# Using Graphic Organizers to Write a Document-Based Essay

**H**ave you ever had to practice for a sporting event or a ballet recital? It takes a tremendous amount of hard work, patience, and coaching. Athletes spend most of their time practicing and preparing for that big day. Using a graphic organizer for the document-based essay is like a football player lifting weights at practice or a ballerina stretching at the barre before a recital. Though these athletes could never use these techniques during a football game or a dance recital, they are a great way to prepare for the main event.

This chapter is designed to help you prepare for your main event, writing a document-based essay for the assessment. Very often, it is difficult for students to begin the writing process. The purpose of a graphic organizer is to help you overcome this difficulty by organizing your information into various categories and charts. Each graphic organizer has been created to take you through the writing process step by step. Think of the graphic organizers as the practice before the main event. Though you may use the graphic organizers to help you with the writing process, it is unlikely that you will ever be provided with one when you are taking an assessment exam. Never solely rely on the graphic organizers to write your essays. They should be used to coach you in the writing process. After you have written your first few essays, try to write an essay without using the graphic organizers.

# ► GRAPHIC ORGANIZER 1—THE INFORMATIONAL CHART

Is the information in your notebook organized by subject or topic to make it easier when doing your homework or studying for an exam? When you arrange your notebook by subject or topic, it is much easier to complete your homework or study for an exam. The information is right at your fingertips. There is no need to search for it, and there is no worry about not including important information. Just as it is important to keep the information in your notebook organized, it is also important to keep the information for your DBQ organized. Because there is so much information included in the DBQ essay, it is easy to forget to include certain requirements. Many times, students will not remember to include important document information or outside information.

The purpose of this graphic organizer is to help you organize and link together both your document information and your outside information to meet the requirements of the DBQ. Before you begin to write down your information, try to think of a topic for each document. Try to develop the topic of the document using a limited amount of words. You do not want to write the topic in sentence form. For example, if the theme of your document-based essay is the U.S. Constitution, and the first document is the First Amendment, write your topic as "First Amendment." There is no need to write, "The topic of this document is the First Amendment." This will help you later when you begin to form your thesis statement. Remember, document information refers to the information given to you in the document. Your answers to the scaffolding questions can help you complete the document information section in this graphic organizer. You may also use any key words from the document you feel are helpful or important. Outside information refers to your knowledge about the topic. When writing your outside information, you are demonstrating your understanding of the topic. You may not use information contained in the documents as part of your outside information. You can obtain your outside information by using your class notes or by researching the topic. When using this particular graphic organizer, there is no need to write using complete sentences. At this point in the writing process, you are just jotting down ideas. As long as you understand your notes, you may just write down important facts or words.

| Document Number | Document Information | Outside Information |
| --- | --- | --- |
| Document 1<br>Topic _____ | | |
| Document 2<br>Topic _____ | | |
| Document 3<br>Topic _____ | | |

| Document Number | Document Information | Outside Information |
|---|---|---|
| Document 4 Topic _____ | | |
| Document 5 Topic _____ | | |
| Document 6 Topic _____ | | |
| Document 7 Topic _____ | | |
| Document 8 Topic _____ | | |
| Document 9 Topic _____ | | |

## ▶ GRAPHIC ORGANIZER 2—THE ESSAY LAYOUT

Do your parents ever hassle you about cleaning your room? Is your locker in school neatly arranged? Whether cleaning your room or arranging your school locker in a neat and orderly fashion, you need one very important skill: ORGANIZATION. Sometimes it is difficult to keep track of the many items we possess. If your books are not organized in your locker, or your clothes are not organized in your closets, being prepared can be a complicated task. The same is true when writing an essay. If your essay is unorganized, your writing will not be clear, therefore causing you to receive a lower score on the assessment rubric.

The purpose of this graphic organizer is to help you structure your information to write the rough draft of your essay. Now that you have organized your document information and outside information, it is time to put your writing to work. Though the thesis statement can be written at the end of your introductory paragraph, it is our suggestion that before you begin to write your introduction, you formulate your thesis statement. Since your essay will evolve around your thesis statement, it is imperative that you make this the first step of the writing process. After you have developed and written down your thesis statement, you may begin writing your introduction. We will discuss, in detail, how to write the DBQ essay in Chapter 6. When completing this graphic organizer, we suggest that you write using complete sentences.

After you finish writing your rough draft, you may also use this graphic organizer to proofread and edit your work. Remember, even though they appear to be different paragraphs in this graphic organizer, your document information and your outside information may be included in the same paragraph. Since you must cite the document you are using in your essay, a space has been provided after the document information for you to write down the number of the document you are referring to. You should cite the document you are using right after you write your document information. Do not cite the document after you have written your outside information. These pieces of information are separate pieces of information and should be treated as such. Be sure that each new body paragraph begins with a topic sentence. The topic sentence should refer back to your thesis statement. Your conclusion should wrap up your essay by summarizing the main points and relating these points to the thesis statement.

## Introduction

_____

_____

_____

_____

_____

## Thesis Statement

_____

_____

_____

_____

**Document Information**

_____

_____

_____

_____

**Document #** _____

**Outside Information**

_____

_____

_____

_____

**Document Information**

_____

_____

_____

_____

**Document #** _____

**Outside Information**

_____

_____

_____

_____

_____

**Document Information**

_____

_____

_____

_____

_____

**Document # _____**

**Outside Information**

_____

_____

_____

_____

_____

**Document Information**

_____

_____

_____

_____

**Document #** _____

**Outside Information**

_____

_____

_____

_____

**Document Information**

_____

_____

_____

_____

**Document #** _____

**Outside Information**

_____

_____

_____

_____

**Conclusion**

_____

_____

_____

_____

_____

The following is an example of how the Essay Layout graphic organizer would be used when writing an essay. The theme of this particular essay is the U.S. Constitution.

**Introduction**

In the beginning, God created heaven and earth; in the beginning of our newly founded nation, god-fearing men created the U.S. Constitution. After the American Revolution, the American people were caught in a period of political turmoil and social upheaval. Those who remained loyal to Great Britain faced social disgrace and were not considered by the Patriots to be American citizens. Everyone was engrossed in a period of economic depression. As a result of the war, the new nation faced an enormous amount of debt. Trade between states was extremely difficult and was almost nonexistent with foreign nations. The Articles of Confederation almost caused the decay of the new nation. The founding fathers were faced with a tremendous burden. They were not only compelled to create a new government which bonded the states into one body, but they also were compelled to protect the rights of the American citizens. The document born out of this determination to make the new nation a success was the U.S. Constitution. Federalists argued that the document protected the rights of the people in its entirety. Anti-Federalists argued that they would not ratify the new document until a Bill of Rights was included. For the success of the new nation and to secure the existence of the Constitution, the Bill of Rights became the first ten amendments added to the new Constitution.

## Thesis Statement

The ways in which the U.S. Constitution protects the rights of American citizens are by granting them freedom of religion, speech, press, and assembly, the right to vote, protection against illegal search and seizure, allowing a process for amendments, and protecting the rights of those accused of a crime.

## Document Information

The first way in which the U.S. Constitution protects the rights of the American citizens is by granting them freedom of religion, speech, and press. According to the First

Amendment, Congress cannot create a national religion or church. Every American citizen has the right to speak and write freely. We as Americans, are also entitled to hold public meetings and to ask the government to correct any wrongs.

**Document #  3**

## Outside Information

In 1969, the case of _Tinker v. Des Moines School District_ came before the Supreme Court. John and Mary Beth Tinker were students in the district who decided to wear black armbands in protest of the Vietnam War. The district made a rule that said that no armbands could be worn to school. Anyone who wore an armband would be suspended. The Supreme Court ruled that the armbands symbolized their protest of the war. Therefore, suspending the students for wearing armbands was unconstitutional because it violated their First Amendment right to freedom of speech.

## Document Information

The second way in which the U.S. Constitution protects the rights of the American citizens is by giving them the right to vote. When the Constitution was first established, only white males over the age of 21 who owned property could vote. The Fifteenth Amendment guarantees that the right to vote cannot be denied because of your race, color, or past history of being a slave. This amendment gave African Americans the right to vote. In addition to the Fifteenth Amendment, the Nineteenth Amendment extended the right to vote to women. This amendment stated that the right to vote cannot be denied because of sex.

Document # <u>7 and 8</u>

## Outside Information

The Fifteenth Amendment was ratified in 1870. This amendment allowed African American males age 21 and older to vote. This amendment infuriated women because they were not included and thrilled Republicans because they could now obtain the African American vote. Though African Americans were legally allowed to vote, they were still prevented from voting in many ways. For instance, many African Americans were poor and could not afford to pay the required poll tax. This was a tax that eligible citizens were required to pay before voting. Literacy tests also prevented African Americans from voting because they had little to no education. One certain way to prevent African Americans from voting was the grandfather clauses passed by some states. These clauses stated that people who did not pass the literacy test could vote only if their forefathers had been eligible to do so prior to Reconstruction. The first time women demanded equal rights and addressed the issue of voting was in 1848 at the Seneca Falls Convention in New York. Two pioneers in the women's rights movement were Elizabeth Cady Stanton and Susan B. Anthony. Activists in this movement fought for equal rights for women in the areas of education, labor, and religion. Before 1920, women in the United States were denied the right to vote. During the Progressive Era, women's suffrage was a major reform movement.

## Document Information

The third way in which the U.S. Constitution protects the rights of the American citizens is by protecting them against illegal search and seizure. The Fourth Amendment states that no American citizen can have his/her property taken, searched, or seized without a written order from a judge. In order for a judge to issue such a warrant, probable cause must exist. When determining probable cause, one must consider whether or not the search will produce evidence relating to a crime. The warrant must also specifically state the place to be searched and the items to be seized. Any items seized beyond those listed in the warrant cannot be used as evidence in court.

**Document #  4**

## Outside Information

The case of New Jersey v. T.L.O. was brought before the Supreme Court. T.L.O. was a student in a New Jersey high school who was suspected of smoking in school. School officials seized her purse and searched the contents. Evidence indicating that she was smoking marijuana was found in her purse. Not only had T.L.O. broken a school law, she had committed a criminal act. The school officials then called the police, who arrested T.L.O. T.L.O.'s lawyers argued that the evidence found in her purse could not be entered as evidence against her since the way in which it was obtained violated her Fourth Amendment rights. The Supreme Court ruled in favor of the State of New Jersey, saying that school officials had the right to search T.L.O.'s purse because they were insuring the safety of other students and maintaining law and order in the school.

**Document Information**

The fourth way in which the U.S. Constitution protects the rights of the American citizens is by providing a process by which the Constitution can be amended. This process can occur in two different ways. One way in which an amendment can begin is by a proposal being made by two-thirds of both houses of Congress. The other way in which an amendment can begin is by a proposal from two-thirds of the state legislatures at a national convention. This national convention is called by Congress at the request of the states. In either case, three-fourths of states or conventions in three-fourths of the states must vote to ratify the amendment.

Document # _2_

**Outside Information**

The flexibility of the Constitution to change with the times is found In its ability to be amended. The first time the Constitution was amended was in 1791 when the Bill of Rights was added. The Bill of Rights contains the first ten amendments to the Constitution. Since the Bill of Rights, 17 more amendments have been added for a total of 27 amendments. Each amendment carries its own important significance.

For example, the Fifteenth Amendment abolished slavery in the United States. The Second Amendment gave American citizens the right to bear arms or carry a weapon.

## Document Information

A final example of the way in which the U.S. Constitution protects the rights of the American citizens is by protecting the rights of those accused of a crime. As an American citizen, you cannot be prosecuted for a crime unless you have been indicted or formally accused of the crime by a grand jury. You may not be tried for the same crime twice. You cannot be forced to testify against yourself or give information that would be self-incriminating. You have the right to a fair trial. The government cannot take away your property without paying you an adequate price for it.

**Document # 5**

## Outside Information

In 1966, the case of Miranda v. Arizona was brought before the Supreme Court. Ernesto Miranda was accused of rape in the state of Arizona. His victim identified him in a police lineup and he was arrested. While being interrogated by police, Miranda confessed to the crime. Miranda took his case to the Supreme Court on appeal. He claimed that his Fifth Amendment rights had been violated because he was unaware of the fact that he had the right to remain silent. The court ruled in favor of Miranda. As a result of this case, police officers must inform anyone they arrest of their rights at the time of the arrest.

**Conclusion**

The Constitution is a living document that continues to protect the rights of American citizens today. Whether we are electing an official in a voting booth, participating in a courtroom trial, writing an editorial, or participating in a social movement to advance our liberties, the Constitution is at work, defending and protecting the freedoms our forefathers worked so tirelessly to ensure. It is our duty as American citizens to uphold the laws set forth in this necessary document to ensure peace and prosperity for ourselves and for future generations.

## ► GRAPHIC ORGANIZER 3—THE DBQ CHECKLIST

Have you ever gotten to your math class and forgotten your calculator? Have you ever forgotten a pen for English class or a notebook for social studies? All of these instruments are important to classroom success. A hectic schedule sometimes causes us to be forgetful. If we are not prepared for class, our grades will suffer. The same is true for the DBQ. When writing an essay with a tremendous amount of substance, it is easy to become distracted or to ramble on and forget to include the necessary requirements and different pieces of information that will result in a high rubric score.

The purpose of this graphic organizer is to help you proofread your essay. The DBQ checklist is designed to make sure you include all of the necessary requirements of the DBQ to be successful. When completing the checklist, be sure to proofread every paragraph of your essay, from your introduction to your conclusion. Only place a checkmark next to the item if you have included it in your essay. If the item is not included in your essay, this is your signal to go back and edit your essay. Do not check the item off until you have edited your essay and you are satisfied with the final product. Once you have proofread your essay and edited it, you may now begin writing the final draft of your essay.

*Student Checklist for a DBQ*
   **1.** \_\_\_\_\_The essay includes a strong introduction (does not restate the historical context but shows knowledge of the theme).
   **2.** \_\_\_\_\_The introduction includes a clear thesis statement which completely addresses or answers the task question.
   **3.** \_\_\_\_\_Each body paragraph contains a topic sentence that refers back to the thesis statement.
   **4.** \_\_\_\_\_Most of the documents contained in the DBQ are used in the essay.
   **5.** \_\_\_\_\_The documents are clearly explained and interpreted in the body paragraphs.

6. \_\_\_\_Outside information, which supports the information in the documents, is contained in the body paragraphs.
7. \_\_\_\_The facts and information contained in the essay are accurate.
8. \_\_\_\_The essay includes a strong conclusion, which supports the thesis statement.
9. \_\_\_\_Correct spelling is used.
10. \_\_\_\_Correct grammar is used.

## HOW DO YOU KNOW WHEN YOU HAVE COMPLETED THE CHECKLIST CORRECTLY?

How do you feel after a long day at school or after attending a sporting practice? Very often, you are tired and running out of energy. After spending countless hours interpreting documents and practicing your essay, you will feel as though the checklist is the race to the end. On the contrary, the checklist is the beginning of the editing process. This is why it is important to complete the checklist honestly and accurately. Use the guidelines below to help you complete the checklist and begin the editing process.

1. \_\_\_\_The essay includes a strong introduction (does not restate the historical context, but shows knowledge of the theme).

When writing the introduction, be sure to demonstrate your knowledge of the theme. You may do this by including factual information, powerful words, examples, and when you have the opportunity, a hook (an attention-grabbing sentence or phrase). The following is an example of an introduction for a DBQ on the U.S. Constitution:

In the beginning, God created heaven and earth; in the beginning of our newly founded nation, god-fearing men created the U.S. Constitution. After the American Revolution, the American people were caught in a period of political turmoil and social upheaval. Those who remained loyal to Great Britain faced social disgrace and were not considered by the Patriots to be American citizens. Everyone was engrossed in a period of economic depression. As a result of the war, the new nation faced an enormous amount of debt. Trade between states was extremely difficult and was almost nonexistent with foreign nations. The Articles of Confederation almost caused the decay of the new nation. The founding fathers were faced with a tremendous burden. They were not only compelled to create a new government which bonded the states into one body, but they also were compelled to protect the rights of the American citizens. The document born out of this determination to make the new nation a success was the U.S. Constitution. Federalists argued that the document protected the rights of the people in its entirety. Anti-Federalists argued that they would not ratify the new document until a Bill of Rights was included. For the success of the new nation and to secure the existence of the Constitution, the Bill of Rights became the first ten amendments added to the new Constitution.

2. \_\_\_\_The introduction includes a clear thesis statement which completely addresses or answers the task question.

The thesis statement is the main idea of your essay or the point you are trying to prove in your essay. You may use the task question as well as the documents to create your thesis statement. Observe how the following task question can be transformed into a thesis statement.

**Task Question:** Using the accompanying documents and your knowledge of social studies, discuss ways in which the U.S. Constitution safeguards or protects the rights of American citizens.

**Thesis Statement:** The ways in which the U.S. Constitution protects the rights of American citizens are by granting them freedom of religion, speech, the press, and assembly. It gives them the right to vote, protection against illegal search and seizure, a process for amendments, and protection of the rights of those accused of a crime.

**3.** _____ Each body paragraph contains a topic sentence which refers back to the thesis statement. Each body paragraph should begin with a topic sentence that refers back to the thesis statement. When writing the topic sentence, use transition words to move from one body paragraph to the next. This will keep the reader informed about the main idea of the essay and will help the essay flow smoothly. The following examples are topic sentences for each body paragraph using the U.S. Constitution:

*First Body Paragraph:* The first way in which the U.S. Constitution protects the rights of the American citizens is by granting them freedom of religion, speech, and the press.

*Second Body Paragraph:* The second way in which the U.S. Constitution protects the rights of the American citizens is by giving them the right to vote.

*Third Body Paragraph:* The third way in which the U.S. Constitution protects the rights of the American citizens is by protecting them against illegal search and seizure.

*Fourth Body Paragraph:* The fourth way in which the U.S. Constitution protects the rights of the American citizens is by providing a process by which the Constitution can be amended.

*Fifth Body Paragraph:* The final way in which the U.S. Constitution protects the rights of the American citizens is by protecting the rights of those accused of a crime.

As you can see, by creating your topic sentences and using transition words to write the topic sentences, the essay takes on the appearance of being organized and well planned.

**4.** _____ Most of the documents contained in the DBQ are used in the essay.
As was stated in an earlier chapter, you must use most of the documents contained in the DBQ in your essay. If the essay contains eight documents, at least five of those documents should be discussed in your essay. By using most of the documents in your essay, you are taking on the role of author/historian and demonstrating your ability to work with primary source documents.

**5.** _____ The documents are clearly explained and interpreted in the body paragraphs.
When writing your body paragraphs, you can begin discussing the documents after you have written your topic sentence. While discussing the documents, reflect on the title, the topic, the purpose of the document, and the author's viewpoint, as well as your own point of view. You may use the

chart from the previous chapter to help you. Using a DBQ on the U.S. Constitution, with the Fifth Amendment as one of the documents, your chart would look like this:

## *Amendment 5*

No person shall be held to answer for a capital, or otherwise infamous crime, unless on a presentment or indictment of a grand jury, except in cases arising in the land or naval forces, or in the militia, when in actual service in time of war or public danger; nor shall any person be subject for the same offense to be twice put in jeopardy of life and limb; nor shall be compelled, in any criminal case, to be a witness against himself; nor be deprived of life, liberty, or property, without due process of law; nor shall private property be taken for public use, without just compensation.

HOW TO PREVIEW THE DOCUMENT ▶

| Preview Questions | Answers to Preview Questions |
|---|---|
| What type of document is this? | This document is an excerpt of the Bill of Rights that is contained in the U.S. Constitution. |
| What is the title of the document? | The title of the document is the Fifth Amendment. |
| What is the topic of the document? | The document's topic is about protecting the rights of someone who is accused of a crime. |

| Reading Strategy Questions | Answers to Reading Strategy Questions |
| --- | --- |
| Who is the writer? | The writers are the framers of the Constitution. |
| What is the time period? | The time period is 1791, the year in which the Bill of Rights was added to the U.S. Constitution. |
| What are the main points of the document? | The main points of the document are: <br> a. No person can be prosecuted for a crime unless they are indicted (formally accused) by a grand jury. <br> b. You cannot be tried for the same crime twice. <br> c. You cannot be forced to testify against yourself or give information which would be self-incriminating. <br> d. You have the right to a fair trial. <br> e. The government cannot take away your property without paying you an adequate price for it. |
| What is the writer's viewpoint? | The framers of the Constitution believed that those who were accused of a crime were entitled to certain rights that the government could not take away. |
| What is the purpose of the document? | The purpose of the document is to specifically discuss those rights to which those who are accused of a crime are entitled. |
| What key words or phrases will help you understand the document? | The key words that will help me to understand the document are: <br> a. indictment <br> b. grand jury <br> c. jeopardy <br> d. deprived <br> e. compensation |

| Reading Strategy Questions | Answers to Reading Strategy Questions |
|---|---|
| Is the evidence for the writer's viewpoint of the topic correct? | Yes, the writer's viewpoint of the topic is correct. |
| Do you think the writer has omitted any important topic information, and if so, what? | The writer has not omitted any important topic information. |
| Do you agree or disagree with the writer's viewpoint? | I agree with the views the framers of the Constitution included in the Fifth Amendment. It is important, that as American citizens, we are entitled to certain rights when we are accused of a crime. |

6. ____Outside information, which supports the information in the documents, is contained in the body paragraphs.

When you are writing your outside information, be sure the information you are writing is in some way related to the document you discussed previously. Outside information refers to information that is not contained in the document, but relates to the topic of the document. Using the informational chart will help you to link your document information with your outside information. The following is an example of how to link your outside information with your document information using the informational chart and the following documents from the U.S. Constitution.

# The U.S. Constitution Documents

## DOCUMENT 1: THE PREAMBLE (INTRODUCTION)

We the people of the United States, in order to form a more perfect Union, establish justice, insure **domestic** (home) **tranquility** (peace), provide for the common defense, promote the general **welfare** (good), and secure the blessings of **liberty** (freedom) to ourselves and our posterity, do ordain and establish this Constitution for the United States of America.

## DOCUMENT 2: ARTICLE 5

The Congress, whenever two-thirds of both houses shall deem it necessary, shall propose **amendments** (changes) to this Constitution, or, on the application of the **legislatures** (law-making bodies: the legislature of the United

States government consists of the House of Representatives and the Senate) of two-thirds of the several states, shall call a **convention** (meeting) for proposing amendments, which, in either case, shall be **valid** to all intents and purposes, as part of this Constitution, when **ratified** (approved) by the legislatures of three-fourths of the several states, or by conventions in three-fourths thereof, as the one or the other mode of ratification may be proposed by the Congress; provided that no amendments which may be made prior to the year 1808 shall in any manner affect the first and fourth clauses in the Ninth Section of the First Article; and that no state, without its consent shall be **deprived** of its equal **suffrage** (vote) in the Senate.

## DOCUMENT 3: AMENDMENT 1

Congress shall make no law respecting an establishment of religion, or prohibiting the free exercise thereof; or **abridging** (limiting) the freedom of speech, or of the press; or the right of the people peaceably to assemble, and to **petition** (ask) the government for a **redress** (correction) of **grievances** (wrongs).

## DOCUMENT 4: AMENDMENT 4

The right of the people to be **secure** (safe) in their persons, houses, papers, and effects, against unreasonable searches and seizures, shall not be **violated**; and no **warrants** (an order from a judge authorizing an arrest or a search an seizure) shall issue but upon **probable** (likely) cause, supported by **oath** (promise) or **affirmation** (confirmation), and particularly describing the place to be searched, and the persons or things to be seized.

## DOCUMENT 5: AMENDMENT 5

No person shall be held to answer for a **capital** (capital crimes are punishable by death), or otherwise **infamous crime** (crimes which carry a prison sentence or cause you to lose some of your rights), unless on a presentment or **indictment** (formal accusation) of a grand jury, except in cases arising in the land or naval forces, or in the militia, when in actual service in time of war or public danger; nor shall any person be subject for the same offense to be twice put in **jeopardy** (danger) of life and limb; nor shall be **compelled** (forced), in any criminal case, to be a witness against himself; nor be **deprived** of life, liberty, or property, without due process of law; nor shall private property be taken for public use, without just **compensation** (payment).

## DOCUMENT 6: AMENDMENT 10

The powers not **delegated** (given to) to the United States by the Constitution, nor **prohibited** (forbidden) by it to the states, are **reserved** (set aside) to the states respectively, or to the people.

## DOCUMENT 7: AMENDMENT 15

The right of citizens of the United States to vote shall not be denied or **abridged** (limited) by the United States or any state on the account of race, color, or previous condition of **servitude** (slavery).

## DOCUMENT 8: AMENDMENT 19

The right of citizens of the United States to vote shall not be denied or **abridged** (limited) by the United States or by any state on the account of sex.

| Document Number | Document Information | Outside Information |
|---|---|---|
| Document 1<br>Topic: The Preamble | The Preamble explains the purpose of the Constitution. The purpose of our government is to create unity among the states, ensure that we have peace within our nation, provide a way to defend ourselves from our enemies, provide for the well-being of the people, and give us and future generations the ability to live as we choose, so long as it is within the laws created by the people. | During the American Revolution, many patriots believed that Great Britain was not concerned with providing for the well-being of its citizens in the colonies. They believed that the only reason Great Britain came to the aid of the colonists in the French and Indian War was because they were protecting their own economic interests. It was not customary for the mother country to concern herself with domestic disputes within the colonies. In all of the disputes between the colonists and the Indians, it was the colonists who were responsible for defending themselves. Great Britain also passed a series of acts or laws that greatly infringed upon the freedom of the colonists. One such act was the Quartering Act, which stated that the colonists were required to house British soldiers. After the revolution was over, the Articles of Confederation provided for a loose alliance of the independent states. This loose alliance almost |

| Document Number | Document Information | Outside Information |
|---|---|---|
| Document 1<br>Topic: The Preamble<br>(continued) | | caused the decay of the new nation. There was social upheaval within the colonies as well. Loyalists were viewed as traitors and were treated as such. When the framers of the Constitution were writing the document, they wanted the American people to know that the intent of the new government was to secure their liberties, not deprive them of their liberties. The words "We the people" indicate that this document was created by the people for the people. It was not created by a monarch who could once again infringe upon their rights. |
| Document 2<br>Topic: Amending the Constitution | The Constitution can be amended or changed. This process can occur in two different ways. One way in which an amendment can be started is by a proposal being made by two-thirds of both houses of the Congress. The other way in which an amendment can be started is by a proposal from two-thirds of the state legislatures at a national convention. Congress calls this national convention at the request of the states. In either case, three-fourths of the states or conventions in three-fourths of the states must vote to ratify the amendment. | The flexibility of the Constitution to change with the times is found in its ability to be amended. The first time the Constitution was amended was in 1791 when the Bill of Rights was added. The Bill of Rights contains the first ten amendments to the Constitution. Since the Bill of Rights, 17 more amendments have been added for a total of 27 amendments. Each amendment carries its own important significance. For example, the Fifteenth Amendment abolished slavery in the United States. The Second Amendment gave American citizens the right to bear arms or carry a weapon. |

| Document Number | Document Information | Outside Information |
|---|---|---|
| Document 3<br>Topic: Freedom of speech, religion, the press, and assembly. | 1. Congress cannot create a national religion or church.<br>2. Every American citizen has the right to speak and write freely.<br>3. American citizens have the right to hold public meetings.<br>4. The American public has the right to ask the government to correct any wrongs. | In 1969, the case of *Tinker v. Des Moines School District* came before the Supreme Court. John and Mary Beth Tinker were students in the district who decided to wear black armbands in protest of the Vietnam War. The district made a rule that said that no armbands could be worn to school. Anyone who wore an armband would be suspended. The Supreme Court ruled that the armbands symbolized their protest of the war. Therefore, suspending the students for wearing armbands was unconstitutional because it violated their First Amendment right to freedom of speech. |
| Document 4<br>Topic: Illegal search and seizure | No American citizen can have his/her property searched or seized without a written order from a judge. In order for a judge to issue such a warrant, probable cause must exist. When determining probable cause, one must consider whether or not the search will produce evidence that relates to a crime. The warrant must also specifically state the place to be searched and the items to be seized. Any items seized beyond those listed in the warrant cannot be used as evidence in court. | The case of *New Jersey v. T.L.O.* was brought before the Supreme Court. T.L.O. was a student in a New Jersey high school who was suspected of smoking in school. School officials seized her purse and searched the contents. Evidence indicating that she was smoking marijuana was found in her purse. Not only had T.L.O. broken a school law, she had committed a criminal act. The school officials called the police who arrested T.L.O. T.L.O.'s lawyers argued that the evidence found in her purse could not be entered as evidence against her since the way in which it was obtained violated her Fourth Amendment rights. The Supreme Court ruled in favor of the State of New Jersey saying that school |

| Document Number | Document Information | Outside Information |
|---|---|---|
| Document 4<br>Topic: Illegal search and seizure (continued) | | officials had the right to search T.L.O.'s purse because they were ensuring the safety of other students and maintaining law and order in the school. |
| Document 5<br>Topic: Rights of the accused | 1. No person can be prosecuted for a crime unless they are indicted (formally accused) by a grand jury.<br>2. You cannot be tried for the same crime twice.<br>3. You cannot be forced to testify against yourself or give information that would be self-incriminating.<br>4. You have the right to a fair trial.<br>5. The government cannot take away your property without paying you an adequate price for it. | In 1966, the case of *Miranda v. Arizona* was brought before the supreme court. Ernesto Miranda was accused of rape in the state of Arizona. His victim identified him in a police lineup and he was arrested. While being interrogated by police, Miranda confessed to the crime. Miranda took his case to the Supreme Court on appeal. He claimed that his Fifth Amendment rights had been violated because he was unaware of the fact that he had the right to remain silent. The court ruled in favor of Miranda. As a result of this case, police officers must inform any one they arrest of their rights at the time of the arrest. |
| Document 6<br>Topic: Powers given to the states | The power of the federal government is limited. The states can assume any power which is not specifically given to the federal government in the Constitution. The only way the states cannot assume these powers is if the Constitution forbids them to have it. | The powers of the states and the federal government are divided by the system of federalism. This system gives the states the right to create and maintain schools, conduct elections, establish local government, set marriage and driving laws, and set the legal age for the consumption of alcohol. The federal government has the right to declare war, make treaties, establish post offices, coin money, and establish armed forces. |

| Document Number | Document Information | Outside Information |
| --- | --- | --- |
| Document 7<br><br>Topic: Right to vote for African Americans | Your right to vote cannot be denied because of your race, color, or past history of being a slave. This amendment gave African Americans the right to vote. | The Fifteenth Amendment was ratified in 1870. This amendment allowed African American males age 21 and older to vote. This amendment infuriated women because they were not included, and thrilled Republicans because they could now obtain the African American vote. Though African Americans were legally allowed to vote, they were still prevented from voting in many ways. For instance, many African Americans were poor and could not afford to pay the required poll tax. This was a tax that eligible citizens were required to pay before voting. Literacy tests also prevented African Americans from voting because they had little to no education. One certain way to prevent African Americans from voting was the grandfather clauses passed by some states. These clauses stated that people who did not pass the literacy test could vote only if their forefathers had been eligible to do so prior to Reconstruction. |
| Document 8<br><br>Topic: Women's Suffrage | Your right to vote cannot be denied because of your sex. This amendment gave women the right to vote. | The first time women demanded equal rights and addressed the issue of voting was in 1848 at the Seneca Falls Convention in New York. Two pioneers in the women's rights movement were Elizabeth Cady Stanton and Susan B. Anthony. Activists in this movement fought for equal rights for women in the areas of education, labor, and religion. Before 1920, women in the United States |

| Document Number | Document Information | Outside Information |
| --- | --- | --- |
| Document 8<br>Topic: Women's Suffrage<br>(continued) | | were denied the right to vote.<br>During the Progressive Era,<br>women's suffrage was a major<br>reform movement. |

**7.** _____The facts and information contained in the essay are accurate.

When writing information in your essay, the facts and information *must* be accurate. Using inaccurate information will result in a lower rubric score. For example, saying that Thomas Jefferson wrote the U.S. Constitution is incorrect. Thomas Jefferson wrote the Declaration of Independence, not the Constitution. When writing your practice essays, you may use different reference books such as textbooks and encyclopedias to check the accuracy of your information. However, when taking an assessment exam, you will *not* have access to these reference materials. The operative word here is *STUDY*. Familiarize yourself with the various topics you have been taught so you won't be caught empty-handed. Be prepared. Don't wait until you are taking the exam to concern yourself with being knowledgeable about the topics.

**8.** _____The essay includes a strong conclusion, which supports the thesis statement.

When you give someone a gift, it is usually neatly wrapped and has a bow attached to the package. Think of the conclusion as the bow to your essay. It is the finishing touch that completes the package. When writing your conclusion, refer back to the question and the thesis statement. Summarize the main points of your essay. In the introduction, you attempted to catch the reader's attention by including a hook. In the conclusion, try to have the subject make a lasting impression on the reader. View the conclusion below on the U.S. Constitution.

The Constitution is a living document that continues to protect the rights of American citizens today. Whether we are electing an official in a voting booth, participating in a courtroom trial, writing an editorial, or participating in a social movement to advance our liberties, the Constitution is at work, defending and protecting the freedoms our forefathers worked so tirelessly to ensure. It is our duty as American citizens to uphold the laws set forth in this necessary document to ensure peace and prosperity for ourselves and for future generations.

**9.** _____Correct spelling is used.

If you were trying out for a basketball team, how would you present yourself? If you arrive wearing high heels and a dress, you would almost certainly not have much luck in getting a chance to play. The coach would probably believe that you were not serious about playing. Sometimes, appearance can be everything. The same is true about your essay. By not checking and correcting your spelling, you are allowing the reader to believe that the appearance of your essay is not important to you. Some spelling errors are very common. Here are some examples:

Example #1:    Recieve (wrong)
               Receive (correct)

When using words where the letters i and e are next to each other, always remember this rule: *i* comes before *e*, except after *c* and when sounding like *a* as in neighbor and weigh.

Example #2:    Dessert
               Desert

Always remember dessert is what you have after dinner. An easy way to remember this is that you can often have strawberry shortcake for dessert. Dessert contains the letter **s** twice. The beginning letters of the words *strawberry* and *shortcake* are the letter *s*. A desert is an arid piece of land where there is limited water and vegetation.

These are just a couple of examples to show you how easy it is to make a spelling error. Even adults when writing or typing are capable of making spelling errors. The best way to correct your spelling is by using a dictionary. If you know the first three letters of the word, or you can sound it out, you can successfully find the word in a dictionary. If you have access to a computer, you can use the spell check function to correct your spelling. As you continue to use these helpful tools, your spelling will improve. You want to give your essay the appearance it deserves. Remember, sometimes appearance is everything!

**10.** _____Correct grammar is used.

Correct grammar usage is just as important to your essay as correct spelling. When you proofread your essay, be sure your sentence structure is correct. Each sentence should begin with a capital letter. A subject (noun or pronoun being spoken about) and a predicate (verb) are required to write a complete sentence. A punctuation mark should be used to indicate the completion of the sentence. If your sentence does not contain these vital pieces, it is considered a sentence fragment. Look at the examples below to see the difference between a sentence and a sentence fragment.

Example:    The school officials. (sentence fragment)
            The school officials then called the police. (sentence)

Notice that the fragment, "The school officials," has a subject (officials) but does not have a verb to complete the action of the sentence. The sentence, "The school officials then called the police," contains a verb (called) that completes the action of the sentence.

When writing a sentence, you must also be aware of comma usage. Commas are used to separate items in a series. Read the following examples to see how a comma can be used in a sentence.

A comma can be used to separate an introductory phrase from the rest of the sentence. If a comma is not used, the sentence is grammatically incorrect.

Example #1:   During the Progressive Era women's suffrage was a major reform movement. (grammatically incorrect)
During the Progressive Era, women's suffrage was a major reform movement. (grammatically correct)

Since the word **during** is a preposition, "During the Progressive Era" is a prepositional phrase. Therefore, it must be separated by a comma.

A comma may also be used to separate information in a sentence.

Example #2:   The First Amendment guarantees your right to freedom of religion speech press and assembly. (grammatically incorrect)
The First Amendment guarantees your right to freedom of religion, speech, press, and assembly. (grammatically correct)

Separating information makes it much easier for the reader to read and understand.

Many times, when we are writing, we commonly misuse words in a sentence. The sentences below will give you an idea of how to correctly use a word that sounds the same, but has a different spelling and meaning.

1.  **a** and **an**
    *a*—used before words beginning with a consonant
    *an*—used before words beginning with a vowel
    A.  The founding fathers wanted to write *a* Constitution that would protect the rights of all Americans.
    B.  As *an* American citizen, we are entitled to certain rights.

2.  **accept** and **except**
    *accept*—to take or receive
    *except*—with the exclusion of
    A.  Americans *accept* the Constitution as the law of the land.
    B.  All states are on the continent of North America, *except* Hawaii.

3.  **affect** and **effect**
    *affect*—to influence
    *effect*—outcome or result
    A.  Slavery issues were destined to greatly *affect* the relationship between the northern states and the southern states.
    B.  One *effect* of the Industrial Revolution was the development of factories in the United States.

4.  **allowed** and **aloud**
    *allowed*—permitted
    *aloud*—using a speaking voice
    A.  During the American Revolution, the colonists were not *allowed* to make laws for themselves.
    B.  The President reads his speech *aloud* when he gives the State of Union Address.

**5. already** and **all ready**

    *already*—indicates or specifies time

    *all ready*—finished, complete

    A.  The revolution was **already** underway when the Declaration of Independence was written.

    B.  The soldiers were **all ready** to fight in the war.

**6. alright** and **all right**

    *alright*—correct, satisfactory

    *all right*—variant spelling of alright

    A.  It is **alright** to practice the religion of your choice in America.

    B.  **"All right,"** the congressman said to his constituents. "I will voice your concerns during our next meeting."

**7. anyone** and **any one**

    *anyone*—any person or thing

    *any one*—one person or thing in particular

    A.  **Anyone** who disagreed with the policies of Great Britain was considered to be a traitor.

    B.  **Any one** person, who is a citizen of the United States, is protected by the Constitution.

**8. buy** and **by**

    *buy*—to purchase something

    *by*—indicates action

    A.  The patriots had a difficult time trying to **buy** supplies.

    B.  World War II was won **by** the Allied powers.

**9. capital** and **capitol**

    *capital*—official city in a state

    *capitol*—government building

    A.  Albany is the **capital** of New York.

    B.  Senators meet in the **capitol** building.

**10. choose** and **chose**

    *choose*—to select

    *chose*—selected (past tense)

    A.  During the American Revolution, the colonists were forced to **choose** sides.

    B.  The patriots **chose** to break away from Great Britain.

**11. hear** and **here**

    *hear*—to listen to

    *here*—specifies a place

    A.  We were able to **hear** the cries of the wounded soldiers.

    B.  Immigrants came over **here** seeking a better way of life.

**12. hole** and **whole**

    *hole*—an opening

    *whole*—complete

    A.  The Confederate soldier's uniform, displayed in the museum, was riddled with ***holes.***

    B.  By reading the ***whole*** Constitution, we can understand the way our government was designed to function.

**13. its** and **it's**

    *its*—belonging to

    *it's*—contraction for "it is"

    A.  The Constitution, in ***its*** entirety, is the supreme law of the land.

    B.  ***It's*** the right of the people to elect officials to represent them.

**14. knew** and **new**

    *knew*—past tense of know

    *new*—recent

    A.  The patriots ***knew*** they risked execution if they lost the revolutionary war.

    B.  The soldiers needed ***new*** supplies.

**15. know** and **no**

    *know*—to understand

    *no*—not permitted

    A.  ***No*** person can violate the rights of another.

    B.  Did the framers of the Constitution ***know*** the important contribution they were making to American history?

**16. lead** and **led**

    *lead*—to direct

    *led*—past tense of lead

    A.  Robert E. Lee was chosen to ***lead*** the Confederate army.

    B.  George Washington ***led*** the Continental army.

**17. loose** and **lose**

    *loose*—free, not bound

    *lose*—misplace, not to win

    A.  The Articles of Confederation created a ***loose*** alliance among the states.

    B.  Abraham Lincoln was determined to preserve the Union and not ***lose*** the southern states to secession.

**18. meat** and **meet**

    *meat*—edible part of an animal

    *meet*—come together

    A.  The colonists' diet consisted of ***meat*** and vegetables.

    B.  The members of the Continental Congress agreed to ***meet*** in Philadelphia, Pennsylvania.

**19. past** and **passed**

   *past*—previous, beforehand

   *passed*—approved

   A.  In the ***past***, the United States has come into conflict with other nations.

   B.  In 1971, a law was ***passed*** lowering the voting age to 18.

**20. right** and **write**

   *right*—correct

   *write*—to form letters or words

   A.  Americans have the ***right*** to practice their religion freely.

   B.  Soldiers would ***write*** letters home to their families.

**21. scene** and **seen**

   *scene*—a view or picture

   *seen*—past participle of see

   A.  Paul Revere illustrated the ***scene*** of the Boston Massacre in his famous engraving.

   B.  The Vietnam War was the first war to be ***seen*** on American television.

**22. than** and **then**

   *than*—instead of

   *then*—indicates time

   A.  Rather ***than*** accepting Great Britain's restrictive policies, the patriots chose to fight.

   B.  First, John C. Calhoun was the Vice President of the United States. He ***then*** became a senator from South Carolina.

**23. there, their,** and **they're**

   *there*—indicating a place

   *their*—indicates ownership of something

   *they're*—contraction for "they are"

   A.  ***There*** have been 27 amendments to the Constitution.

   B.  The framers of the Constitution were interested in protecting ***their*** freedom.

   C.  ***They're*** supporters of the U.S. Constitution.

**24. threw** and **through**

   *threw*—past tense of throw—an act of motion

   *through*—by means of, among, or between

   A.  The Bostonians ***threw*** rocks and stones at the British soldiers.

   B.  The British soldiers wandered ***through*** the wilderness in search of the patriot rebels.

**25. to, too,** and **two**

   *to*—indicates direction

   *too*—also

   *two*—the number after one

   A.  What freedoms were given ***to*** the slaves after the Civil War?

   B.  Women wanted the right to vote ***too***.

   C.  There are more than ***two*** amendments to the Constitution.

**26.** **weak** and **week**

    *weak*—not strong

    *week*—length of time, seven days

    A.  Many immigrants were **weak** when they arrived at Ellis Island.

    B.  **Week** after **week**, women worked to support the war effort.

**27.** **wear** and **where**

    *wear*—to have or carry on the body

    *where*—location or place

    A.  It was not uncommon for a woman to **wear** a petticoat in colonial times.

    B.  **Where** did the Battle of Bunker Hill take place?

**28.** **which** and **witch**

    *which*—what one, the one that

    *witch*—a person who has magical powers

    A.  The assembly line, **which** allowed workers to mass produce cars, was introduced by Henry Ford in 1913.

    B.  The Salem **Witch** trials occurred in 1692.

**29.** **who** and **whom**

    *who*—the subject in a sentence

    *whom*—person or thing receiving the action in a sentence

    A.  **Who** wrote the Declaration of Independence?

    B.  For **whom** was the Treaty of Paris written?

**30.** **who's** and **whose**

    *who's*—contraction for "who is"

    *whose*—possessive of who, shows ownership

    A.  **Who's** responsible for initiating World War I?

    B.  Orville and Wilbur Wright were two bicycle mechanics **whose** invention of the plane revolutionized transportation in America.

**31.** **your** and **you're**

    *your*—possessive of you

    *you're*—contraction of "you are"

    A.  The U.S. Constitution protects **your** individual rights.

    B.  **You're** entitled to freedom of speech by the First Amendment.

There are many ways in which you can become confused with word usage. In order to give your essay the proper appearance, it is important to make sure your word usage is correct.

# How to Write a Document-Based Essay

When you wake up in the morning, how do you plan your day? When you go on vacation, how do you plan your itinerary? When you play a sport, how do you plan your strategy for success? If you haven't noticed, the key word in all of these questions is *PLAN!* When you begin the writing process, the most important step is the planning step, and this chapter is designed to help you with just that. You will be able to take the necessary steps you need to take to write your document-based essay. The following steps are a plan of action to help you write the DBQ.

## ► SIX STEPS TO WRITING A DOCUMENT-BASED ESSAY

1. Read the theme, historical context, and task question for the DBQ. Create a list of facts that you know about the topic. This list can be used for your outside knowledge.
2. List *all* information given in the documents.
   A. What type of document is this? (political cartoon, journal, artwork, quote, graph, diagram)
   B. Who is the author? What is the time period?
   C. What is the author's point of view?
   D. Circle keywords, phrases, or pictures.
   E. Answer the scaffolding questions that follow each document.

3. Using the information contained in **most** of the documents, create your **thesis statement.** The thesis statement answers the task question.

> - Remember, *most* means using more than half of the documents.
> - The thesis statement is the main idea of your essay or the point you are trying to prove to the reader.

4. Underline the keywords given in the historical context. You may use these words in your introduction. Your introduction **must** be in your own words and contain your thesis statement. Write your introduction.
5. Write a paragraph for each piece of information contained in your thesis statement. Use information from the document—as well as your outside information—in your paragraphs to support your thesis statement.
6. Write a conclusion. In your conclusion, restate your thesis, give evidence that supports your thesis, and summarize the main points of your essay.

## HOW DO I KNOW I HAVE FOLLOWED THE STEPS CORRECTLY?

**Step 1—Read the theme, historical context, and task question for the DBQ. Create a list of facts about the topic. This list can be used for your outside knowledge.**

For practice, review the following theme, historical context, and task question for a DBQ on the U.S. Constitution.

**Theme:** The U.S. Constitution

**Historical Context:** After the American Revolution, the Articles of Confederation governed the new nation. This new government created a loose alliance of the newly independent states. Many Americans were suspicious of a central government, fearing that power concentrated in a central government could threaten their freedom. The creation of a weak central government almost led to the failure of the new nation. Under the Articles of Confederation, Congress could not regulate trade between the states or with foreign nations, nor did they have the power to tax. As inflation began to rise and the country entered a period of economic distress, the leaders of the new nation realized the need for a new form of government, one that would be stronger than the Articles of Confederation, yet balance authority in an attempt to protect the rights of American citizens. During the Constitutional Convention of 1787, the U.S. Constitution was born. This powerful document was designed to equally delegate power between the federal and state governments, while at the same time, protect American citizens from tyranny. This new government would never be able to abuse its power and infringe upon the rights of its citizens the way Great Britain infringed upon the rights of the colonists.

**Task:** Using the following documents and your knowledge of social studies, explain how the U.S. Constitution protects or safeguards the rights of American citizens.

Based on this information and subject, a list of facts can be written. The following list is a model for you to use. When you take a test that requires you to write a DBQ, you should come prepared with information like this in order to write this list of outside information. Of course, you usually can't bring notes or books so you need to study the facts well in advance.

*Facts Related to the U.S. Constitution:*

1. The Articles of Confederation called for a weak central government.

2. Federalism is the division of power between the states and the national government. Delegated powers are those given only to the federal government (national government). Only the federal government can declare war, coin money, and make treaties. Reserved powers are those given to the state governments. The state governments can establish schools, conduct elections, and establish local governments. Concurrent powers are those given to both the federal and state governments. Both the federal and state governments can tax, borrow money, and provide for the public welfare.

3. The Constitution divided the U.S. Government into three branches: executive, judicial, and legislative.

4. A system of checks and balances was put into place to prevent any one branch of government from becoming too powerful.

5. The executive branch consists of the President, the Vice President, and the President's cabinet or advisors. The President is elected for a four-year term and can serve only two consecutive terms. The job of the executive branch is to carry out or execute the laws passed by Congress. The executive branch can check or limit the legislative branch by vetoing a law passed by Congress. The executive branch can check or limit the judicial branch by appointing Supreme Court justices.

6. The legislative branch consists of two houses: the House of Representatives and the Senate. The legislative branch is also referred to as Congress. Senators are elected for a six-year term. Representatives are elected for a two-year term. The job of the legislative branch is to make the laws that govern the country. The legislative branch can check the executive branch by overriding the President's veto by a two-thirds vote. The legislative branch also has the power of impeachment. The House of Representatives would bring charges against the President, and the Senate would hold the trial. If the President were found guilty, he would be removed from office. The legislative branch can check the judicial branch by confirming or approving the appointment of a Supreme Court justice. There are no term limits in the legislative branch.

7. The judicial branch consists of the Supreme Court. There are nine justices on the Supreme Court. The job of the Supreme Court is to interpret the Constitution. The Supreme Court checks the legislative branch and the executive branch by the power of judicial review. They can declare a law passed by Congress or an act of the President as unconstitutional. Supreme Court justices are appointed for life. Some famous Supreme Court cases are *Marbury v. Madison*, which established judicial review, *Miranda v. Arizona*, which scrutinized the Fifth Amendment, *Brown v. the Board of Education of Topeka, Kansas*, which examined the issue of school segregation, and *Roe v. Wade*, which examined the issue of abortion.

8. There was much debate over the ratification of the Constitution. The Federalists argued for a strong central government and claimed that the Constitution, as it was written, provided a strong central government while protecting the rights of the states and their citizens. The Anti-Federalists argued against the ratification of the Constitution. They believed that the Constitution, as it was written, gave more power to the national government than the states. The major concern of the Anti-Federalists

was that this powerful document did not contain a Bill of Rights. They wanted the basic freedoms of the people listed in the Constitution. They did not want to encounter the tyranny that had existed under British rule.

9. The Bill of Rights became the first ten amendments to the Constitution. These amendments listed the basic freedoms of the American people, such as freedom of speech, freedom of religion, the right to bear arms, protection against self-incrimination, the right to a trial by jury, and protection against illegal search and seizure. The Constitution has been an effective document for over 200 years because of its flexibility. Through the amendment process, we are able to add and delete legislation to meet the needs of changing times.

10. In order to adopt the Constitution, nine of the thirteen states had to vote to ratify. Delaware was the first state to vote to ratify the Constitution. On June 21, 1788, New Hampshire became the ninth state to vote to ratify the Constitution. Rhode Island was the last to vote to ratify. It was important for all states to agree on ratification to unify the states and ensure the success of the new government. The Bill of Rights was added to the Constitution in 1791. The U.S. Constitution is the supreme law of the land.

The creation of this list does not necessarily mean that you must use all of this information in your essay. Once you have read and selected the documents you want to include in your essay, you may use this list to incorporate outside information into your essay. Your outside information should in some way relate to the information contained in the documents you have chosen to use. It is important that you create this list **before** you view the documents. Sometimes understanding the difference between document information and outside information becomes confusing after you have viewed the documents. By creating a list of facts about the theme or topic, you can eliminate the confusion about the two pieces of required information.

**Step 2—List *all* information given in the documents.**
  A. **What type of document is this? (political cartoon, journal, artwork, quote, graph, diagram)**
  B. **Who is the author? What is the time period?**
  C. **What is the author's point of view?**
  D. **Circle keywords, phrases, or pictures.**
  E. **Answer the scaffolding questions that follow each document.**

When trying to interpret the documents, it is important that you view the entire document. Pay attention to detail because it has been included for a reason! Circle anything in the document that you feel is important. Pay attention to the author's point of view. There was a specific intent when the document was written. Do you agree or disagree with their point of view? The answer to this question may affect the way you develop your thesis statement. What is the time period of the document? Is it a piece written when the actual event took place or is someone commenting on the event at a later time? Just as it is imperative for you to list your outside information, it is also imperative that you list your document information. Listing the information in the document will enable you to interpret and understand the purpose of the document better. This in turn will help you write a more effective essay. Use the charts from Chapter 4 on reading and previewing a document to help you. After you have previewed and read the documents, you must answer the scaffolding questions below the document. When you answer the scaffolding questions, you must write your answers in complete sentences. Only include the required information in your answer. **DO NOT** include outside information in your answers to the scaffolding questions. This may cause you to go off on a tangent and not answer the question correctly. Your answers to the scaffolding questions will demonstrate your ability to interpret the document. If your information or interpretation is incorrect, you will lose points on the rubric.

**Step 3—Using the information contained in most of the documents, create your thesis statement by answering the question given in the task.**

Imagine trying to bake a cake without a recipe or assembling a model without a list of instructions. These documents are necessary to give you proper guidance and direction. Think of your thesis statement as the recipe or the instructions for your essay. The thesis statement is the main idea of your essay. This statement clearly tells the reader your point of view. Just as a baker must have a recipe or a model airplane must have a set of instructions, your essay *must* include a thesis statement. Creating the thesis statement can be as simple as using the topics of the documents contained in the DBQ to answer the question presented in the task.

**Step 4—Underline the keywords given in the historical context. You may use these words in your introduction. Your introduction must be in your own words and contain your thesis statement. Write your introduction.**

When you begin writing your introduction, you want to introduce the reader to the topic. You may use keywords in the historical context to help you. If you are having trouble, create sentences using the keywords. Try to connect the sentences so they relate to one another and give the reader an understanding of the theme. Writing a strong introduction will give you a higher score on the rubric. If you simply recopy the historical context as your introduction, you will lose points.

**Step 5—Write a paragraph for each piece of information contained in your thesis statement. Use information from a document—as well as outside information—in your paragraph to support your information.**

After you have written your introduction and your thesis statement, you must begin to write the body of your essay. To create this section of your essay, you should know the following:

- The body of your essay should contain the information given in your thesis statement.
- Each body paragraph must contain a topic sentence.
- Transition words should be used to advance the reader from one paragraph to the next.
- Each body paragraph must contain document information, as well as outside information, which relates to the information given in the topic sentence.
- It is in the body of your essay that you demonstrate your ability to correctly interpret the documents.
- The stronger your body paragraphs, the higher your score on the rubric.

**Step 6—Write a conclusion. In your conclusion, restate your thesis, give evidence that supports your thesis, and summarize the main points of your essay.**

Remember the analogy that was used in Chapter 5 about writing a conclusion? The conclusion is the finishing touch to your essay, just as a bow is the finishing touch to a package. Since a package would not look complete without a bow, your essay is not complete without a conclusion. In your conclusion, you should restate your thesis. This brings the reader back to the main idea or position you took in your essay. By giving evidence that supports your thesis and summarizing the main points of your essay, you are proving your position. When you write your introduction, you want to include an interesting idea or fact that will hook the reader into the essay. When you write your conclusion, you want to include an interesting idea or fact that will leave a lasting impression on the reader.

## ▶ WRITING THE THESIS STATEMENT

What steps do you take before you begin to bake a cake or build a model? Usually, you would read the list of ingredients for baking a cake, or the directions for building a model. Before you can begin to complete these tasks, you must first understand what is expected of you. A good thesis statement is as important to an essay as a list of ingredients is to a recipe or a set of directions is to building a model. The thesis statement is the main idea or your purpose for writing the essay. Before you can begin your essay, you must know what it is you're going to write about. When forming the thesis statement, you must look at the task question and the documents. The task question will explain the important information that is to be included. The documents will be used as evidence to support your thesis statement. Organizing the documents by topic will also help you to formulate your thesis statement. Formulating the thesis statement can be as simple as using the documents to answer the task question. Use the chart like the one below when you begin to write your thesis statement.

```
HOW TO FORMULATE YOUR THESIS STATEMENT  ▶
```

| Thesis Development | Your Response |
|---|---|
| Purpose of the Thesis Statement (Answer to the Task Question) | |
| Document Topics | |
| Thesis Statement | |

Observe how the chart could be used when writing a thesis statement for the U.S. Constitution. For our purpose, we will use seven documents from the U.S. Constitution.

## DOCUMENT 1: ARTICLE 1, SECTION 2

The House of Representatives shall be composed of members chosen every second year by the people of the several states, and the *electors* (voters) state shall have the qualifications requisite for electors of the most numerous branch of the state legislature.

## DOCUMENT 2: ARTICLE 1, SECTION 3

The Senate of the United States shall be composed of two senators from each state chosen by the legislature thereof, for six years, and each senator shall have one vote.

## DOCUMENT 3: ARTICLE 1, SECTION 7

Every bill which shall have passed the House of Representatives and the Senate shall, before it becomes a law, be presented to the President of the United States; if he approves, he shall sign it, but if not, he shall return it, with his objections, to that house in which it shall have originated, who shall enter the objections at large on their journal, and proceed to reconsider it. If after such reconsideration, two-thirds of that house shall agree to pass the bill, it shall be sent, together with the objections, to the other house, by which it shall likewise be reconsidered, and, if approved by two-thirds of that house, it shall become a law. But in all such cases the votes of both houses shall be determined by yeas and nays, and the names of the persons voting for and against the bill shall be entered on the journal of each house respectively. If any bill shall not be returned by the President within ten days (Sundays excepted) after it shall have been presented to him, the same bill shall be a law, in like manner as if he had signed it, unless the Congress by their adjournment prevent its return, in which case it shall not be a law.

## DOCUMENT 4: ARTICLE 2, SECTION 1

The executive power shall be vested in a President of the United States of America. He shall hold his office during the term of four years, and together with the Vice President, chosen for the same term, be elected as follows:

Each state shall appoint, in such manner as the legislature thereof may direct, a number of electors, equal to the whole number of Senators and Representatives to which the state may be entitled in the Congress; but no Senator or Representative, or person holding an office or trust or profit under the United States, shall be appointed as an elector.

## DOCUMENT 5: ARTICLE 3, SECTION 1

The judicial power of the United States shall be vested in one Supreme Court, and in such inferior courts as the Congress may from time to time ordain and establish. The judges, both of the Supreme and inferior courts, shall hold their offices during good behavior, and shall, at stated times, receive for their services a compensation, which shall not be diminished during their continuance in office.

## DOCUMENT 6: ARTICLE 2, SECTION 4

President, Vice President, and all civil officers of the United States, shall be removed from office on impeachment for, and conviction of treason, bribery, or other high crimes or misdemeanors.

## DOCUMENT 7: ARTICLE 5

The Congress, whenever two-thirds of both houses shall deem it necessary, shall propose amendments to this Constitution, or, on the application of the legislatures of two-thirds of the several states, shall call a convention for proposing amendments, which, in either case, shall be valid to all intents and purposes, as part of this Constitution, when ratified by the legislatures of three-fourths of the several states, or by conventions in three-fourths thereof, as the one or the other mode of ratification may be proposed by the Congress; provided that no state, without its consent, shall be deprived of its equal suffrage in the Senate.

**SAMPLE CHART BASED ON DOCUMENTS 1–7** ▶

**Theme:** The U.S. Constitution
**Task Question:** How does the U.S. Constitution safeguard or protect the rights of American citizens?

| Thesis Development | Your Response |
|---|---|
| Purpose of the Thesis Statement: (Your thesis statement answers the task question.) | To demonstrate how the U.S. Constitution protects or safeguards the rights of American citizens. |
| Document Topics | Document 1—term for a Representative<br>Document 2—term for and number of Senators<br>Document 3—how a bill becomes a law<br>Document 4—term and election of a President and Vice President<br>Document 5—establishment of federal courts<br>Document 6—impeachment<br>Document 7—the amendment process |

| Thesis Development | Your Response |
|---|---|
| Thesis Statement | The U.S. Constitution safeguards or protects the rights of American citizens by specifically stating the term length for the President, Vice President, Senators, and Representatives, as well as establishing an amendment and impeachment process. |

Notice how the topics of the documents were used to create the thesis statement by answering the task question. In this particular thesis statement, Documents 1, 2, 4, 6, and 7 were used. Remember, you must use **most** of the documents in your essay. Since there were seven documents included in the DBQ, you must include at least four of the documents in your essay. Therefore, five document topics are mentioned in the sample thesis statement.

Your thesis statement can also be longer than one sentence. That means that you do not have to mesh your information together in one sentence. Look at the following example to see how a thesis statement using the same documents can be made into more than one sentence.

### Sample Thesis Statement:

The establishment of terms for various officials of the U.S. Government safeguards the American people against tyranny. The ability to impeach and amend provided by the U.S. Constitution further ensures a protection of American rights and freedoms.

Notice how you can get your position across applying different language to the same concepts.

## ▶ BEGINNING STEPS

Now let's take a look at writing thesis statements for a variety of themes. The themes are:

- European Exploration
- Colonial America
- The American Revolution
- Westward Expansion
- The Civil War
- The Progressive Era

**Theme:** European Exploration

**Task:** Write an essay in which you explain three ways in which European exploration affected the lives of the Native Americans.

| Thesis Development | Your Response |
|---|---|
| Purpose of the Thesis Statement: (Your thesis statement answers the task question.) | To describe how European exploration affected the lives of the Native Americans. |
| Document Topics | Document 1—conversion of Native Americans to Christianity<br>Document 2—abuse of Native Americans<br>Document 3—diseases<br>Document 4—Columbian exchange<br>Document 5—transportation |
| Thesis Statement | European exploration affected the lives of the Native Americans through the spread of diseases, the Columbian exchange, and the modes of transportation they used. |

Once again, observe that the topics of most of the documents (three out of five) were used in the thesis statement.

The thesis statement could also be written this way:

The Columbian exchange introduced both the Europeans and the Native Americans to a wide variety of goods and livestock. The spread of diseases and introduction of new technology both helped and hindered the Native American way of life.

**Theme:** Colonial America

**Task:** Write an essay in which you explain why many people wanted to migrate to the colonies.

| Thesis Development | Your Response |
|---|---|
| Purpose of the Thesis Statement: (Your thesis statement answers the task question.) | To explain why many people wanted to migrate to the colonies. |
| Document Topics | Document 1—freedom of religion<br>Document 2—economic advancement<br>Document 3—indentured servants<br>Document 4—slavery<br>Document 5—democracy |
| Thesis Statement | Many people migrated to the colonies in search of religious freedom, economic advancement, and democracy. |

In writing this thesis statement, three out of five document topics are used.

The thesis statement could also be written this way:

As economic conditions in England worsened and the demand for labor in the colonies increased, many people began to migrate to the colonies in search of a better way of life. These new immigrants came seeking religious freedom, economic advancement, and a chance to live as free individuals. Many immigrants, however, migrated as indentured servants or slaves to meet the demand for additional labor.

**Theme:** The American Revolution

**Task:** Write an essay in which you explain whether or not the American colonists were justified in breaking away from Great Britain.

| Thesis Development | Your Response |
|---|---|
| Purpose of the Thesis Statement: (Your thesis statement answers the task question.) | To explain whether or not the American colonists were justified in breaking away from Great Britain. |
| Document Topics | Document 1—Proclamation of 1763 Document 2—the Stamp Act Document 3—Boston Massacre Document 4—Declaration of Independence Document 5—Intolerable Acts Document 6—Boston Tea Party Document 7—Townshend Acts |
| Thesis Statement | The American colonists were justified in breaking away from Great Britain because of the Proclamation of 1763, the Stamp Act, the Boston Massacre, the Intolerable Acts, and the Townshend Acts. |

In writing this thesis statement, four of the seven document topics are used.

The thesis statement could also be written this way:

British tyranny began with the issuance of the Proclamation of 1763. Further tyrannical acts such as the Stamp Act, the Boston Massacre, the Intolerable Acts, and the Townshend Acts justified the colonists' desire to declare their own independence. With the writing and acceptance of the Declaration of Independence, the colonists explained and justified the reasons for their necessary separation from the mother country.

**Theme:** Westward Expansion

**Task:** Write an essay in which you discuss the factors that enabled Americans to expand westward.

| Thesis Development | Your Response |
|---|---|
| Purpose of the Thesis Statement: (Your thesis statement answers the task question.) | To discuss the factors that enabled Americans to expand westward. |
| Document Topics | Document 1—large quantities of inexpensive land<br>Document 2—Indian removal<br>Document 3—Union Pacific Railroad<br>Document 4—Erie Canal<br>Document 5—manifest destiny<br>Document 6—gold rush<br>Document 7—cattle and cotton growing in Texas |
| Thesis Statement | The factors that enabled Americans to expand westward were Indian removal, the Erie Canal, the Union Pacific Railroad, and the gold rush. |

In writing this thesis statement, four of the seven documents are used.

The thesis statement can also be written this way:

Many Americans were encouraged to move west as a result of advances in transportation, such as the Erie Canal and the Union Pacific Railroad. This new development in transportation allowed both goods and people to be transported to western areas of the country. The desire for gold and the fact that Indian removal policy opened more territory for anxious settlers caused expansion in the west to become more attractive.

Use the charts on the Civil War and the Progressive Era to write a thesis statement. First, you are to write the purpose of your thesis statement. Then, try to write two thesis statements. The first should just simply respond to the task. The second should demonstrate your fluency as a writer.

**Theme:** The Civil War
**Task:** Write an essay in which you discuss the affects of slavery on African Americans.

| Thesis Development | Your Response |
|---|---|
| Purpose of the Thesis Statement: (Your thesis statement answers the task question.) | |
| Document Topics | Document 1—Fugitive Slave Law<br>Document 2—slave codes<br>Document 3—abusive treatment of slaves by their masters<br>Document 4—Underground Railroad<br>Document 5—abolitionist movement<br>Document 6—poor living conditions of slaves<br>Document 7—Dred Scott decision |
| Thesis Statement | |

First, write the purpose of your thesis statement in the box provided. Then, write your thesis statement in the Thesis Statement box by simply answering the task. Be sure to include most of the document topics (more than half) when you write your thesis statement. After you have written your simple thesis statement, try to write a more fluent thesis, which demonstrates that you can go beyond simply responding to the task.

The thesis statement can also be written this way:

_____

_____

_____

_____

**Theme:** The Progressive Era

**Task:** Write an essay in which you explain the issues the Progressives wanted to reform in an attempt to bring about change in American society.

| Thesis Development | Your Response |
| --- | --- |
| Purpose of the Thesis Statement: (Your thesis statement answers the task question.) | |
| Document Topics | Document 1—child labor<br>Document 2—women's suffrage<br>Document 3—Sherman Anti-Trust Act<br>Document 4—Prohibition<br>Document 5—poor conditions in a meatpacking factory |
| Thesis Statement | |

First, write the purpose of your thesis statement in the box provided above. Then, write your thesis statement in the Thesis Statement box by simply answering the task. Be sure to include most of the document topics (more than half) when you write your thesis statement. After you have written your simple thesis statement, try to write a more fluent thesis, which demonstrates that you can go beyond simply responding to the task.

The thesis statement can also be written this way:

_____

_____

_____

_____

As you can see, the creation of the thesis statement can be as simple or as complex as you want it to be. By writing a more fluent, thorough thesis statement, you will improve your score on the rubric.

## ▶ WRITING THE INTRODUCTION

When you meet someone for the first time, how do you introduce yourself? What do you want your new friend or acquaintance to know about you? Sometimes, first impressions can be lasting ones. Similarly, when you write your introduction, you are introducing the reader to your essay. Your introduction can leave a lasting impression about the rest of your essay. If you are introduced to someone you consider boring or unappealing, chances are you will not want to know more about that person. However, if you encounter someone who is exciting and interesting, you will probably be very enthused to learn more about this person. The same is true with your essay. If you write an introduction that is monotonous and uninformative, chances are you will immediately lose the reader's interest. On the other hand, if you capture the reader's attention immediately, it is very likely the reader will be eager to continue on. When writing your introductory paragraph, you should include the following:

- the theme of the essay
- interesting facts or ideas about the theme
- a hook or an attention-grabbing sentence or phrase
- your point of view about the theme
- the thesis statement

If you are having trouble writing the introduction, you may use keywords from the historical context to help you. Observe how keywords from the historical context on the U.S. Constitution are used to write an introduction.

**Theme:** The U.S. Constitution
**Task:** How does the U.S. Constitution safeguard or protect the rights of American citizens?

**Historical Context:** After the American Revolution, the Articles of Confederation governed the new nation. This new government created a loose alliance of the newly independent states. Many Americans were suspicious of a central government, fearing that power concentrated in a central government could threaten their freedom. The creation of a weak, central government almost led to the failure of the new nation. Under the Articles of Confederation, Congress could not regulate trade between the states or with foreign nations, nor did they have the power to tax. As inflation began to rise and the country entered a period of economic distress, the leaders of the new nation realized the need for a new form of government, one that would be stronger than the Articles of Confederation, yet balance authority in an attempt to protect the rights of American citizens. During the Constitutional Convention of 1787, the U.S. Constitution was born. This powerful document was designed to equally delegate power between the federal and state governments, while at the same time, protect American citizens from tyranny. This new government would never be able to abuse its power and infringe upon the rights of its citizens the way Great Britain infringed upon the rights of the colonists.

The first step after reading the historical context is to underline and highlight the keywords.

**Historical Context:** After the <u>American Revolution</u>, the <u>Articles of Confederation</u> governed the new nation. This new government created a loose alliance of the newly <u>independent</u> states. Many Americans were <u>suspicious</u> of a <u>central government</u>, fearing that power concentrated in a central government could threaten their freedom. The creation of a <u>weak</u> central government almost led to the <u>failure</u> of the <u>new nation</u>. Under the Articles of Confederation, <u>Congress</u> could <u>not</u>

regulate <u>trade</u> between the states or with foreign nations, nor did they have the power to <u>tax</u>. As <u>inflation</u> began to rise and the country entered a period of <u>economic distress</u>, the leaders of the new nation realized the need for a new form of government, one which would be stronger than the Articles of Confederation, yet <u>balance authority</u> in an attempt to <u>protect</u> the rights of American citizens. During the <u>Constitutional Convention of 1787,</u> the <u>U.S. Constitution</u> was born. This powerful document was designed to equally delegate power between the federal and state governments, while at the same time, protect American citizens from <u>tyranny</u>. This new government would never be able to <u>abuse</u> its power and <u>infringe</u> upon the <u>rights</u> of its citizens the way <u>Great Britain</u> infringed upon the rights of the colonists.

Now that you have underlined your keywords, your introductory paragraph can take shape.

### First Sample Introduction Using the Historical Context:

The Articles of Confederation governed the new nation after the American Revolution. At this time, many people were suspicious of a central government. Each state wanted to be independent. Because the central government was so weak, the new nation almost ended in failure. Congress could not tax or regulate trade. Inflation was a problem and the economy was in distress. The nation's leaders realized the need for a new government. During the Constitutional Convention of 1787, the U.S. Constitution was written. The purpose of this Constitution was to balance the authority between the states and the national government to protect the rights of the American people. The American people did not want to face the same abuses as they had under Great Britain. The new government would never be able to abuse its power and infringe upon the rights of the people.

Did you find that introduction interesting or boring? What required elements were missing from that introduction? Even though you can use keywords from the Historical Context, you must use these words to write an exciting introduction. The first sample introduction simply used the words to create sentences. Then the sentences were connected to create an introduction. What's missing? This introduction did not include a thesis statement or a hook. This will result in a lower score on the assessment rubric.

Let's look at another example of an introduction using not only the keywords from the historical context, but a thesis statement and a hook as well.

### Second Sample Introduction Using the Historical Context:

In the beginning, God created heaven and earth; in the beginning of our newly founded nation, god-fearing men created the U.S. Constitution. After the American Revolution, the American people were caught in a period of political turmoil and social upheaval. Those who remained loyal to Great Britain faced social disgrace and were not considered by the Patriots to be American citizens. Everyone was engrossed in a period of economic depression. As a result of the war, the new nation faced an enormous amount of debt. Trade between states was extremely difficult and was almost nonexistent with foreign nations. The Articles of Confederation almost caused the decay of the new nation. The founding fathers were faced with a tremendous burden. They were not only compelled to create a new government which bonded the states into one body, but they also were compelled to protect the rights of the American citizens. The document born out of this determination to make the new nation a success was the U.S. Constitution. Federalists argued that the document protected the rights of the people in its entirety. Anti-Federalists argued that they would not ratify the new document until a Bill of Rights was included. For the success of the new nation and to secure the existence of the Constitution, the Bill of Rights became the first ten amendments added to the new Constitution. The U.S. Constitution protects the rights of American citizens by granting them freedom of religion, speech, press, and assembly. People of all races and genders are guaranteed the right to vote. We, as Americans, are protected against illegal search and seizure. Even those accused of committing a crime have rights, which are protected by the U.S. Constitution. The flexibility and power of the Constitution is seen in the amendment process.

Notice how the hook in the first sentence was able to immediately grab the reader's attention. The second sample introduction is stronger and more effective than the first. Naturally, it is the one you'd prefer to read. Now let's take a look at another example of an introduction.

**Theme:** The American Revolution
**Task:** Write an essay in which you explain whether or not the colonists were justified in breaking away from Great Britain.

**Historical Context:** During the years 1763–1776, there were a series of events that created conflict between the American colonies and Great Britain. Since the beginning of their existence, the colonies had always had a voice in government and were able to contribute to their economic success without any interference from Great Britain. The American colonists believed Great Britain was creating and enforcing laws, which violated the rights of the colonists. The colonists took the position that not having a voice in the British Parliament was unjust. Great Britain believed her colonies should be loyal subjects, since it was Great Britain who was supporting and protecting the colonies. The differing points of view between Great Britain and the American colonies led to a series of conflicts between the two. The ultimate result of this conflict was the termination of the relationship between the colonies and the mother country and the emergence of a new nation, the United States of America.

Now let's follow the first step after reading the historical context and underline and highlight the keywords.

**Historical Context:** During the years <u>1763–1776</u>, there were a series of events that created <u>conflict</u> between the <u>American colonies</u> and <u>Great Britain</u>. Since the beginning of their existence, the colonies had always had a <u>voice</u> in <u>government</u> and were able to <u>contribute</u> to their <u>economic success</u> without any <u>interference</u> from Great Britain. The American colonists believed Great Britain was <u>creating</u> and <u>enforcing laws</u>, which <u>violated</u> the <u>rights</u> of the colonists. The colonists took the position that not having a voice in the British <u>Parliament</u> was <u>unjust</u>. Great Britain believed her colonies should be <u>loyal</u> subjects, since it was Great Britain who was <u>supporting</u> and <u>protecting</u> the colonies. The <u>differing</u> points of view between Great Britain and the American colonies led to a series of conflicts between the two. The ultimate result of this conflict was the <u>termination</u> of the <u>relationship</u> between the colonies and the mother country and the <u>emergence</u> of a new nation, the United States of America.

Based on the keywords that you underlined, an introduction like the one below can be written.

***First Sample Introduction for the American Revolution Using Historical Context:***

The years 1763–1776 were ones of conflict between the American colonies and Great Britain. Since the colonies always had a say in government, they did not believe Great Britain had the right to begin creating and enforcing laws for them. The laws passed by Parliament were unjust and violated the rights of the colonists. The fact that Great Britain supported and protected the colonies did not mean they had the right to abuse them. The American colonists were justified in breaking away from Great Britain because of the Proclamation of 1763, the Stamp Act, the Boston Massacre, the Intolerable Acts, and the Townshend Acts.

Though this introduction contains the author's point of view, the theme, and a thesis statement, it is lacking an enormous amount of detail and does not contain a hook. The use of a hook and the addition of detail would greatly improve this introduction. Not only would it make the theme more appealing to the reader, it would make the reader interested enough to want to read the rest of the essay. Read the sample introduction below. Do you see the difference?

***Second Sample Introduction:***

If the shot heard 'round the world had fallen on deaf ears, where would America be today? The relationship between the American colonists and Great Britain soured between the years 1763 to 1776. After the French and Indian War, Great Britain was faced with the task of paying off the war debt. Since Great Britain entered the war to protect her colonies, she believed they should share the burden of payment. Great Britain also did not want to become involved in any further entanglements with the Indians. All colonial trade and settlement west of the Appalachian Mountains was off limits. Parliament began to issue a series of acts which taxed the colonists in an effort to pay the war debt and infringed upon their rights. Since the beginning of their existence, the establishment of colonial assemblies enabled the colonists to create their own laws and cast their own votes. Taxes had always been a part of colonial life. It was not the issue of taxation that angered the colonists; it was the issue of representation. If the colonists had been granted representation in Parliament, they would have been able to vote on issues concerning taxation and the regulation of trade. Great Britain, on the other hand, believed the colonists should be loyal subjects simply because she provided them with support and protection. But is this enough to justify violating the rights of a certain group? Had the colonists not rebelled, they would have been subjected to an existence engulfed in tyrannical rule. British tyranny began with the issuance of the Proclamation of 1763. Further tyrannical acts such as the Stamp Act, the Boston Massacre, the Intolerable Acts, and the Townshend Acts justified the colonists' desire to declare their own independence. With the writing and acceptance of the Declaration of Independence, the colonists explained and justified the reasons for their necessary separation from the mother country.

What differences do you notice between the first sample introduction and the second? The second sample introduction introduces the reader to the theme, accurately demonstrates the author's point of view, and includes a thesis statement. In addition, the second sample introduction includes supporting details about the theme and a hook to draw the reader into the essay. The use of powerful language also makes this introduction more interesting to the reader.

# NOW IT'S YOUR TURN

Use the following theme, task, and historical context to write your own introduction. Remember to high-light and underline keywords. Include all the necessary information (theme, author's point of view, hook, supporting details, thesis statement, powerful language) to write a strong introduction. The stronger your introduction, the higher your score on the assessment rubric.

**Theme:** The Industrial Revolution

**Task:** Write an essay in which you explain the effects of the Industrial Revolution on American society.

**Historical Context:** Before the nineteenth century, the American economy was based largely on agriculture. As America began to grow and prosper, Americans began to revolutionize the way they carried on their work. New forms of technology were introduced replacing hand tools with machin-ery. Man and animal power was replaced with steam power. The development of such technological advances led to the emergence of factories. The nation was experiencing an economic shift from a farming society to a manufacturing society. As a result of the latest technology, goods could be mass-produced at rapid speeds. The increasing demands of a manufacturing society led to a demand for workers and a rise in urbanization. Women and children began to fill the need for factory work-ers after all available men had been hired, earning money at jobs outside the home rather than home-based employment. People began to migrate from rural areas to urban areas in search of work. The nation as a whole was beginning to change.

After reading the historical context, underline and highlight keywords to help you write your introduction. Remember, your introduction should contain a hook, the theme, a thesis statement, the author's point of view, and as much detail as you need to support your introduction of the theme. Now write an introduction for the Industrial Revolution.

_____

_____

_____

_____

_____

_____

_____

_____

If you feel you are having difficulty, you can always go back to the sample introductions for help. Now try to write another sample introduction using a different theme, task question, and historical context.

**Theme:** The Progressive Era
**Task:** Write an essay explaining the causes and effects of the reforms targeted by the Progressives.

**Historical Context:** The Progressive Era emerged in the late 1800s. The Progressives felt a need for change in American society and worked toward achieving various social, political, and economic reforms. They fought against corruption in government and worked to reduce the power of monopolies. During the Progressive Era, there was a heightened awareness of issues such as women's suffrage and child labor. Muckrakers used journalism as a means to change public opinion on the need for reform. Though African-Americans never truly achieved equal status until the Civil Rights Movement, it was during the Progressive Era that action was first taken against racial discrimination.

After reading the historical context, underline and highlight keywords to help you write your introduction. Once again, your introduction should contain a hook, the theme, a thesis statement, the author's point of view, and as much detail as you need to support your introduction of the theme. Now write an introduction for the Progressive Era.

_____

_____

_____

_____

_____

_____

_____

_____

_____

At this point, you should feel your DBQ muscles flexing. But, if you are still unsure or not satisfied that you are doing the best job, return to the sample introductions for help. The stronger your introduction, the higher your score on the assessment rubric will be.

## ▶ WRITING THE BODY PARAGRAPHS

When you get into your family car to go on a trip, what causes that car to move? The engine is the driving force of the car that enables it to move. The body paragraphs of your essay are like the engine of a car. We all know a car has a front end and a back end, but it's the engine that is the driving force. Just as the engine is the driving force of a car, the body paragraphs are the driving force of the essay. The introduction and conclusion can't go anywhere without the body. Therefore, it is very important that your body paragraphs are presented in an organized manner. There are several ways to organize your body paragraphs. Look at the chart below to choose the best way to organize your body paragraphs.

| Ways to Organize Your Body Paragraphs | Examples of Topics |
|---|---|
| **Compare and Contrast**—inform the reader about similarities and differences. | **Compare and contrast** the role of Great Britain during the American Revolution and the United States during the Vietnam War. |
| **Cause and Effect**—Explain the reasons for (cause) a problem or event and the results of (effect) the problem or event. | What was the **cause and effect** of the Civil Rights Movement? |
| **Order of Importance**—information can be arranged starting with the most important and ending with the least important, or starting with the least important and ending with the most important. | Discuss, in **order of importance**, the reforms proposed by the Progressives. |
| **Chronological Order**—information is arranged according to the time of the event. | Discuss in **chronological order**, the series of events that led to WWI. |
| **Order of Location**—information is arranged according to where things are located in relation to each other. | Describe, by **order of location**, the major battles of WWII. |
| **Problem and Solution**—identify a problem and propose a solution to the problem. | Discuss the **problems** between the United States and the Soviet Union during the Cold War and offer **solutions** to these problems. |

When writing the body of your essay, make sure that it directly relates to your thesis statement. When you learned how to write an effective thesis statement, it was suggested that you use the topics of the documents to write the thesis statement. These topics should now be discussed in the body of the essay. A body paragraph should be devoted to each topic contained in your thesis statement. Each body paragraph should contain a topic sentence. The topic sentence will introduce the reader to the subject of the paragraph. The topics of each of the documents can be used to create the topic sentences in your body paragraphs. Supporting details should follow the topic sentence. The supporting details can be found both in the document information and your outside information. Read the following sample body paragraph on a document containing the First Amendment to the U.S. Constitution.

### Sample Body Paragraph:

The first way in which the U.S. Constitution protects the rights of the American citizens is by granting them freedom of religion, speech, and the press. According to the First Amendment, Congress cannot create a national religion or church. Every American citizen has the right to speak and write freely. We, as Americans, are also entitled to hold public meetings and to ask the government to correct any wrongs.

It is evident from the topic sentence that the purpose of this paragraph is to explain one way in which the U.S. Constitution protects the rights of its citizens. Notice how, after the topic sentence was written, supporting details were added to enhance the information about the topic.

Topic sentences and supporting details can also be used when presenting your outside information in the body paragraphs. Read the body paragraph below, which contains outside information relating to the First Amendment.

In 1969, the case of Tinker v. Des Moines School District came before the Supreme Court. John and Mary Beth Tinker were students in the district who decided to wear black armbands in protest of the Vietnam War. The district made a rule, which said that no armbands could be worn to school. Anyone who wore an armband would be suspended. The Supreme Court ruled that the armbands symbolized their protest of the war. Therefore, suspending the students for wearing armbands was unconstitutional because it violated their First Amendment right to freedom of speech.

The topic sentence informs us that the paragraph will be about the case of *Tinker v. Des Moines School District*. The supporting details in the paragraph gives us information about the court case and relates this information to the First Amendment.

As you continue to write the body of your essay, it is important that the paragraphs, as well as the information contained in them, be connected or linked together to establish continuity within the essay. A great way to connect your paragraphs is by using transition words. Transition words are words that help you to move smoothly from one paragraph to the next. The use of transition words will enable you to present the information in the body of your essay more efficiently. Use the following chart of transition words to help you effectively connect your information and paragraphs to write the body of your essay successfully.

| Role of Transition Words | Transition Words | | |
|---|---|---|---|
| Transition words can indicate a specific time. | about<br>after<br>at<br>today<br>later<br>then | before<br>during<br>first<br>until<br>soon<br>finally | second<br>third<br>yesterday<br>meanwhile<br>next<br>tomorrow |
| Transition words can indicate a specific location. | above<br>around<br>by<br>over<br>beside<br>under<br>against | across<br>along<br>beyond<br>into<br>below<br>inside<br>near | in back of<br>among<br>off<br>in front of<br>beneath<br>throughout<br>over |
| Transition words can be used to compare and contrast things. | otherwise<br>however<br>similarly<br>nevertheless | but<br>still<br>unlike<br>by contrast | on the contrary<br>in spite of<br>conversely |
| Transition words can be used to add information. | again<br>next<br>as well<br>and<br>in addition<br>moreover | also<br>finally<br>another<br>besides<br>specifically<br>furthermore | another<br>along with<br>for instance<br>for example |
| Transition words can be used to compare things | likewise<br>also<br>in either case | similarly<br>in the same way | as |
| Transition words can be used to accentuate a point. | in fact | for this reason | |
| Transition words can be used to summarize. | finally<br>lastly | as a result | therefore |
| Transition words can start the first body paragraph. | First<br>one method | one way | one example |
| Transition words can be used in the middle body paragraphs. | another<br>not only<br>moreover | in addition<br>second<br>then | to next<br>third<br>besides |
| Transition words can be used in the final body paragraph. | a final example<br>a final instance<br>finally | a final method<br>a final way<br>lastly | |

Read the following body paragraphs on the U.S. Constitution to see how transition words connect one paragraph to the next and allow the essay to flow from one topic to the next. The transition words have been underlined and highlighted for you to recognize.

*Sample Body Paragraphs:*

**The first way** in which the U.S. Constitution protects the rights of American citizens is by granting them freedom of religion, speech, and the press. According to the First Amendment, Congress cannot create a national religion or church. Every American citizen has the right to speak and write freely. We, as Americans, are also entitled to hold public meetings and to ask the government to correct any wrongs.

In 1969, the case of *Tinker v. Des Moines School District* came before the Supreme Court. John and Mary Beth Tinker were students in the district who decided to wear black armbands in protest of the Vietnam War. The district made a rule, which said that no armbands could be worn to school. Anyone who wore an armband would be suspended. The Supreme Court ruled that the armbands symbolized their protest of the war. **Therefore,** suspending the students for wearing armbands was unconstitutional because it violated their First Amendment right to freedom of speech.

**The second way** in which the U.S. Constitution protects the rights of the American citizens is by giving them the right to vote. When the Constitution was first established, only white males over the age of 21 who owned property could vote. The Fifteenth Amendment guarantees that the right to vote cannot be denied because of your race, color, or past history of being a slave. This amendment gave African Americans the right to vote. **In addition to** the Fifteenth Amendment, the Nineteenth Amendment extended the right to vote to women. This amendment stated that the right to vote cannot be denied because of sex.

The Fifteenth Amendment was ratified in 1870. This amendment allowed African American males age 21 and older to vote. This amendment infuriated women because they were not included and thrilled Republicans because they could now obtain the African American vote. Though African Americans were legally allowed to vote, they were still prevented from voting in many ways. **For instance,** many African Americans were poor and could not afford to pay the required poll tax. This was a tax that eligible citizens were required to pay before voting. Literacy tests also prevented African Americans from voting because they had little to no education. One certain way to prevent African Americans from voting were the grandfather clauses passed by some states. These clauses stated that people who did not pass the literacy test could vote only if their forefathers had been eligible to do so prior to Reconstruction. The first time women demanded equal rights and addressed the issue of voting was in 1848 at the Seneca Falls Convention in New York. Two pioneers in the women's rights movement were Elizabeth Cady Stanton and Susan B. Anthony. Activists in this movement fought for equal rights for women in the areas of education, labor, and religion. **Before** 1920, women in the United States were denied the right to vote. **During** the Progressive Era, women's suffrage was a major reform movement.

**The third way** in which the U.S. Constitution protects the rights of the American citizens is by protecting them against illegal search and seizure. The Fourth Amendment states that no American citizen can have his or her property taken, searched, or seized without a written order from a judge. In order for a judge to issue such a warrant, probable cause must exist. When determining probable cause, one must consider whether or not the search will produce evidence relating to a crime. The warrant must also specifically state the place to be searched and the items to be seized. Any items seized beyond those listed in the warrant cannot be used as evidence in court.

The case of *New Jersey v. T.L.O.* was brought before the Supreme Court. T.L.O. was a student in a New Jersey high school who was suspected of smoking in school. School officials seized her purse and searched the contents. Evidence indicating that she was smoking marijuana was found in her purse. Not only had T.L.O. broken a school law, she had committed a criminal act. The school officials then called the police, who arrested T.L.O. T.L.O.'s lawyers argued that the evidence found in her purse could not be entered as evidence against her since the way in which it was obtained violated her Fourth Amendment rights. The Supreme Court ruled in favor of the State of New Jersey saying that school officials had the right to search T.L.O.'s purse because they were ensuring the safety of other students and maintaining law and order in the school.

**The fourth way** in which the U.S. Constitution protects the rights of the American citizens is by providing a process by which the Constitution can be amended. This process can occur in two different ways. One way in which an amendment can begin is by a proposal being made by two-thirds of both houses of Congress. The other way in which an amendment can begin is by a proposal from two-thirds of the state legislatures at a national convention. This national convention is called by Congress at the request of the states. **In either case,** three-fourths of states or conventions in three-fourths of the states must vote to ratify the amendment.

The flexibility of the Constitution to change with the times is found in its ability to be amended. The first time the Constitution was amended was in 1791 when the Bill of Rights was added. The Bill of Rights contains the first ten amendments to the Constitution. Since the Bill of Rights, 17 more amendments have been added for a total of 27 amendments. Each amendment carries its own important significance. For example, the Fifteenth Amendment abolished slavery in the United States. The Second Amendment gave American citizens the right to bear arms or carry a weapon.

**A final example** of the way in which the U.S. Constitution protects the rights of the American citizens is by protecting the rights of those accused of a crime. As an American citizen, you cannot be prosecuted for a crime unless you have been indicted or formally accused of the crime by a grand jury. You may not be tried for the same crime twice. You cannot be forced to testify against yourself or give information which would be self-incriminating. You have the right to a fair trial. The government cannot take away your property without paying you an adequate price for it. In 1966, the case of *Miranda v. Arizona* was brought before the Supreme Court. Ernesto Miranda was accused of rape in the state of Arizona. His victim identified him in a police lineup and he was arrested. While being interrogated by police, Miranda confessed to the crime. Miranda took his case to the Supreme Court on appeal. He claimed that his Fifth Amendment rights had been violated because he was unaware of the fact that he had the right to remain silent. The court ruled in favor of Miranda. As a result of this case, police officers must inform any one they arrest of their rights at the time of the arrest.

As you can see, the use of transition words allows both the body paragraphs and the information contained within the body paragraphs to demonstrate your knowledge of the topic effectively by creating a smooth, consistent flow of information. You may use the thesis statement chart to help you organize your body paragraphs according to the topics contained in your thesis statement. By doing so, you will be sure to include all of the necessary documents in your essay. Remember, the use of most of the documents, the incorporation of outside information, a strong introduction, a smooth, consistent flow of information within the body, and a strong conclusion will enable you to raise your score on the assessment rubric.

Use the theme, task question, thesis statement chart, transition word chart, and the following documents to help you write the body paragraphs for an essay on the U.S. Constitution.

**Documents:** Reread the following documents. These were used for your thesis statement earlier in this chapter. Then write your body paragraphs.

## DOCUMENT 1: ARTICLE 1, SECTION 2

The House of Representatives shall be composed of members chosen every second year by the people of the several states, and the *electors* (voters) state shall have the qualifications requisite for electors of the most numerous branch of the state legislature.

## DOCUMENT 2: ARTICLE 1, SECTION 3

The Senate of the United States shall be composed of two senators from each state chosen by the legislature thereof, for six years, and each senator shall have one vote.

## DOCUMENT 3: ARTICLE 1, SECTION 7

Every bill which shall have passed the House of Representatives and the Senate shall, before it becomes a law, be presented to the President of the United States; if he approves, he shall sign it, but if not, he shall return it, with his objections, to that house in which it shall have originated, who shall enter the objections at large on their journal, and proceed to reconsider it. If after such reconsideration, two-thirds of that house shall agree to pass the bill, it shall be sent, together with the objections, to the other house, by which it shall likewise be reconsidered, and, if approved by two-thirds of that house, it shall become a law. But in all such cases the votes of both houses shall be determined by yeas and nays, and the names of the persons voting for and against the bill shall be entered on the journal of each house respectively. If any bill shall not be returned by the President within ten days (Sundays excepted) after it shall have been presented to him, the same bill shall be a law, in like manner as if he had signed it, unless the Congress by their adjournment prevent its return, in which case it shall not be a law.

## DOCUMENT 4: ARTICLE 2, SECTION 1

The executive power shall be vested in a President of the United States of America. He shall hold his office during the term of four years, and together with the Vice President, chosen for the same term, be elected as follows:

Each state shall appoint, in such manner as the legislature thereof may direct, a number of electors, equal to the whole number of Senators and Representatives to which the state may be entitled in the Congress; but no Senator or Representative, or person holding an office or trust or profit under the United States, shall be appointed as an elector.

## DOCUMENT 5: ARTICLE 3, SECTION 1

The judicial power of the United States shall be vested in one Supreme Court, and in such inferior courts as the Congress may from time to time ordain and establish. The judges, both of the Supreme and inferior courts, shall hold their offices during good behavior, and shall, at stated times, receive for their services a compensation, which shall not be diminished during their continuance in office.

## DOCUMENT 6: ARTICLE 2, SECTION 4

President, Vice President, and all civil officers of the United States, shall be removed from office on impeachment for, and conviction of treason, bribery, or other high crimes or misdemeanors.

## DOCUMENT 7: ARTICLE 5

The Congress, whenever two-thirds of both houses shall deem it necessary, shall propose amendments to this Constitution, or, on the application of the legislatures of two-thirds of the several states, shall call a convention for proposing amendments, which, in either case, shall be valid to all intents and purposes, as part of this Constitution, when ratified by the legislatures of three-fourths of the several states, or by conventions in three-fourths thereof, as the one or the other mode of ratification may be proposed by the Congress; provided that no state, without its consent, shall be deprived of its equal suffrage in the Senate.

**Theme:** The U.S. Constitution
**Task Question:** How does the U.S. Constitution safeguard or protect the rights of American citizens?

| THESIS DEVELOPMENT | YOUR RESPONSE |
| --- | --- |
| Purpose of the Thesis Statement: (Your thesis statement answers the Task Question) | To demonstrate how the U.S. Constitution protects or safeguards the rights of American citizens. |
| Document Topics | Document 1—term for a Representative |
| | Document 2—term for and number of Senators |
| | Document 3—how a bill becomes a law |
| | Document 4—term and election of a President and Vice President |
| | Document 5—establishment of federal courts |
| | Document 6—impeachment |
| | Document 7—the amendment process |

| THESIS DEVELOPMENT | YOUR RESPONSE |
| --- | --- |
| Thesis Statement | The U.S. Constitution safeguards or protects the rights of American citizens by specifically stating the term length for the President, Vice-President, Senators, and Representatives, as well as establishing an amendment and impeachment process. |

*Sample Body Paragraphs:*

_____

_____

_____

_____

_____

_____

_____

_____

_____

_____

_____

_____

_____

_____

_____

_____

_____

You are on your way to becoming a successful writer if you have done all of the following. Your score on the assessment rubric will surely reflect all of your hard work.

- Effective transition words should have been used to connect your body paragraphs.
- All required information should have been included.
- The writing should have guided your reader smoothly through the body of your essay while emphasizing the major points of your essay.

## ► WRITING THE CONCLUSION

When writing your conclusion, you want to put the finishing touches on your essay. This is the time to tie up any loose ends or clarify the points made in the body of your essay. You want to make sure the reader completely understands the purpose of your essay. When concluding, you want to remind the readers of the topic. If you are having trouble writing your conclusion, you can

- restate your thesis as the first sentence.
- summarize the main points of your essay.
- state the importance of one of your points.

Just as the hook was used to draw the reader's attention to your essay, the conclusion should provide the reader with a lasting impression about the subject. Read the following conclusion on the U.S. Constitution DBQ.

The Constitution is a living document that continues to protect the rights of American citizens today. Whether we are electing an official in a voting booth, participating in a courtroom trial, writing an editorial, or participating in a social movement to advance our liberties, the Constitution is at work, defending and protecting the freedoms our forefathers worked so tirelessly to insure. It is our duty as American citizens to uphold the laws set forth in this necessary document to assure peace and prosperity for ourselves and for future generations.

Do you see how the author reminded the reader of the importance of the topic by stating specific examples about the Constitution at work today? The author linked the importance of the Constitution from the time period in which it was written to today. Explaining our duties as American citizens to the reader made a lasting impression.

A hook may also be written in the form of a question in your introduction. If this is the case, then you may answer the hook question in your conclusion to bring closure to your essay. Reread the second sample introduction below on the American Revolution. You should be able to see how the hook was written in the form of a question. The hook question has been highlighted and underlined for you.

***If the shot heard 'round the world had fallen on deaf ears, where would America be today?*** The relationship between the American colonists and Great Britain soured between the years 1763 to 1776. After the French and Indian War, Great Britain was faced with the task of paying off the war debt. Since Great Britain entered the war to protect her colonies, she believed they should share the burden of payment. Great Britain also did not want to become involved in any further entanglements with the Indians. All colonial trade and settlement west of the Appalachian Mountains was off limits. Parliament began to issue a series of acts, which taxed the colonists in an effort to pay the war debt and infringed upon their rights. Since the beginning of their existence, the establishment of colonial assemblies enabled the colonists to create their own laws and cast their own votes. Taxes had always been a part of colonial life. It was not the issue of taxation that angered the colonists; it was the issue of representation. If the colonists had been granted representation in Parliament, they would have been able to vote on issues concerning taxation and the regulation of trade. Great Britain, on the other hand, believed the colonists should be loyal subjects simply because she provided them with support and protection. But is this enough to justify violating the rights of a certain group? Had the colonists not rebelled, they would have been subjected to an existence engulfed in tyrannical rule. British tyranny began with the issuance of the Proclamation of 1763. Further tyrannical acts such as the Stamp Act, the Boston Massacre, the Intolerable Acts, and the Townshend Acts justified the colonists' desire to declare their own independence. With the writing and acceptance of the Declaration of Independence, the colonists explained and justified the reasons for their necessary separation from the mother country.

Now let's take a look at how a conclusion to this essay would read if we were to begin writing by answering the hook question.

If the shot heard 'round the world had fallen on deaf ears, we would not enjoy the freedoms we are entitled to as Americans today. We would not be permitted to bear arms, as we were granted this privilege by the Second Amendment. The right to vote for representatives in our government who could shield us against rising taxes would be a dream, not a reality. A system of checks and balances would not exist within our governmental structure to prevent a tyrannical leader or an abuse of power by government officials. We would be under the jurisdiction and control of a government in which we had no recourse against unfair practices. As we enjoy the various freedoms we as Americans so readily accept, we must remember those courageous Patriots, who conscientiously fought for a cause they so fiercely believed in. If it were not for them, we could not celebrate the freedoms we enjoy today.

Notice how the hook question was immediately answered in the first sentence of the conclusion. A combination of supporting details, outside information, and powerful language was used to enhance the answer to the question and to illustrate the importance of the topic to the reader. A lasting impression was made by asking the reader to remember those who fought so ardently to achieve this goal. By further enhancing your information, and creating a lasting impression for the reader, you are working to improve your score on the assessment rubric.

## ▶ Now It's Your Turn

Earlier you were asked to write sample body paragraphs for the U.S. Constitution. Now try to use the main points you made in the body paragraphs, along with the theme and the thesis statement, to write a successful conclusion. This might also be a good time to once again try to develop a hook. You might want to phrase your hook in the form of a question, and answer the question in your conclusion. Use the space below to write your conclusion.

_____

_____

_____

_____

_____

_____

_____

_____

_____

_____

_____

_____

_____

If your conclusion had a hook question with an answer, a summary of the main points made in the essay, and if it left the reader with a lasting impression, you were able to achieve your goal. Your score on the assessment rubric will show this.

You should have a firm grasp of the writing process by the end of this chapter. Remember, to be a successful writer takes hard work and practice. If you do not feel successful with your first piece, use the revision strategies discussed in the next chapter to help you achieve your goal. You may revise your essay as many times as you want during practice. However, on the day of the assessment exam, you will have only one chance to prove your abilities to the reader. With persistence and determination, you will achieve a high score on the assessment rubric and will become a successful author/historian.

CHAPTER

# *Revision Strategies*

**O**ur first words are seldom our best words. When you style your hair, does it look perfect the first time? Or do you turn to the mirror, take another look (from all angles), and redo it until you are perfectly satisfied that it's just right? Well, that's what revision is all about, taking another look and rewriting until you are completely satisfied that you will make a good impression. This chapter is designed to give you strategies that will help you make your original draft better.

We bet that as soon as people invented writing, someone invented the first eraser. We are only human; we make mistakes. Even if we didn't make any mistakes, we could make things better. We are always improving the gas mileage of cars, the speed of computers, and the impact absorption of sneakers. We don't have to look to the present for revision. Take a look at the following well-known document. Yes, The Constitution of the United States of America. Notice the lines through certain portions. Even our founding fathers decided to improve upon a good thing.

# THE FOLLOWING IS AN EXCERPT FROM ARTICLE 1.
## THE LEGISLATIVE BRANCH.

Section 3. Determining Representation

Representatives (~~and direct taxes~~) shall be apportioned among the several states, which may be included within this Union, according to their respective numbers (~~which shall be determined by adding to the whole number of free persons, including those bound to service for a term of years, and excluding Indians not taxed, three-fifths of all other persons.~~) The actual enumeration shall be made within three years after the first meeting of the Congress of the United States, and within every subsequent term of ten years, in such manner as they shall by law direct. The number of Representatives shall not exceed one for every 30,000, but each state shall have at least one Representative; (~~and until such enumeration shall be made, the State of New Hampshire shall be entitled to choose three; Massachusetts, eight; Rhode Island and Providence Plantations, one; Connecticut, five; New York, six; New Jersey, four; Pennsylvania, eight; Delaware, one; Maryland, six; Virginia, ten; North Carolina, five; South Carolina, five; and Georgia, three.~~)

Almost all good writing is revised writing, and good writing places the audience first. Your audience on state exams is most likely someone you don't know and will never meet. It is likely that the person grading your paper has sat through some training sessions learning how to grade papers and will be grading many of the same essays on a particular day. You must keep in mind that it is your job to prove—to this person—that you can write clearly and answer the task questions. The best way to do this is to make sure that your writing targets six basic areas: specificity, continuity, redundancy, introductions and conclusions, vital verbs, and sentence combining. If some of these terms sound like they are beyond you, rest assured. They are explained very clearly in this chapter. Even though you must learn **to read between the lines** in many documents, you must not make the person grading your paper **read between the lines** that you have written. On the contrary, your writing must be crystal clear, no hidden meanings.

Sometimes it is not possible to revise and rewrite the entire essay because of time limits. In that case, you should revise as you write. Learn to put one line through a mistake and insert a caret (∧) in order to add something. This is why **skipping lines** as you write is a good strategy—just in case you need to add information. Above all, make your corrections clear to the reader.

**Target Area 1: Specificity**—Give specific examples and details. Write with specific nouns (*Lord of the Rings*) and verbs (disappear). Writing with vague nouns (person) and verbs (is, am, was, were, be, being) does not give information.

For instance, if you were to report a missing dog, which report do you think would be the most helpful to get your dog back?

> **Report A:** My dog is lost. It is cute and friendly. I love him a lot.
> **Report B:** My six-year-old, male Golden Retriever ran away from his 123 Courtyard Lane home on July 4. He has a very light blond, long-haired coat. He is obedience-trained and responds to the name Dakota. He has a pink nose and a dark one-quarter inch mark on his tongue.

When you give specific details, you help the reader understand better what you are trying to prove. Avoid vague pronouns like he, she, it, and they. Instead, name the person or people. Try to answer the who, what, when, where, why, and how. If the person or people are not named in the document, identify the culture or occupation.

The following is a sentence written to answer a document-based question about the Nile River's effect on the lives of the Egyptians.

> **This sentence lacks specificity:** The people were near the river. (This example is vague. The reader is left wondering who the people were and which river it was.)
>
> **This sentence is very specific:** The **Egyptian** people *settled* along the **Nile** River. (Now, the writer has specifically answered **who** and **where** and has used the strong verb *settled*.)

Following are four examples of paragraphs that answer a particular task question that you might see on a document-based question. Examine each one carefully and highlight the specific details and examples the writer provides. Comments—like the ones given by state assessment readers—are given below each sample.

**Task question:** How does the U.S. Constitution safeguard the rights of American citizens?

### Writer A's Introduction:

The Constitution protects people's rights.

**Comments:** This introduction is weak because it lacks specificity. Which Constitution is it? Which people's rights? Most importantly, the sentence does not answer the task question: **How does the U.S. Constitution safeguard the rights of American citizens?**

Because it is only one sentence, the writer neglects to include necessary background information and document topics.

### Writer B's Introduction:

The documents have views that are for and against the Constitution. Some people were loyal and disloyal to England. This made a difference in who supported the Articles of Confederation and who supported the Constitution.

**Comments:** This introduction is very weak because it does not answer the task question and lacks specificity. What is the issue? Who are the people on both sides of the issue? Which Constitution? What does it have to do with the task question, **How does the U.S. Constitution safeguard the rights of United States citizens?**

### Writer C's Introduction:

The ways in which the U.S. Constitution protects the rights of American citizens are by granting them freedom of religion, speech, press, and assembly, the right to vote, protection against illegal search and seizure, allowing a process for amendments, and protecting the rights of those accused of a crime.

**Comments:** The writer has included only the thesis in this introduction. Although the thesis is quite effective, there is no attempt to explain outside information or gain the reader's interest, two very necessary steps writers need to take in order to receive the highest possible ratings on document-based essays.

*Writer D's Introduction:*

In the beginning, God created heaven and earth; in the beginning of our newly founded nation, god-fearing men created the U.S. Constitution. After the American Revolution, the American people were caught in a period of political turmoil and social upheaval. Those who remained loyal to Great Britain faced social disgrace and were not considered by the Patriots to be American citizens. Everyone was engrossed in a period of economic depression. As a result of the war, the new nation faced an enormous amount of debt. Trade between states was extremely difficult and was almost nonexistent with foreign nations. The Articles of Confederation almost caused the decay of the new nation. The founding fathers were faced with a tremendous burden. They were not only compelled to create a new government which bonded the states into one body, but they also were compelled to protect the rights of the American citizens. The document born out of this determination to make the new nation a success was the U.S. Constitution. Federalists argued that the document protected the rights of the people in its entirety. Anti-Federalists argued that they would not ratify the new document until a Bill of Rights was included. For the success of the new nation and to secure the existence of the Constitution, the Bill of Rights became the first ten amendments added to the new Constitution. The ways in which the U.S. Constitution protects the rights of American citizens are by granting them freedom of religion, speech, press, and assembly, the right to vote, protection against illegal search and seizure, allowing a process for amendments, and protecting the rights of those accused of a crime.

**Comments:** Writer D has written a superb introduction that answers the task question, **How does the U.S. Constitution protect and safeguard the rights of U.S. citizens?** It has elements from writers A, B, and C, and includes specific groups of people and documents in a clear, logical progression that sets the reader up for what's to come in the body paragraphs. The atmosphere of postrevolutionary America is clearly described, the issue of a strong government that also protects individuals is presented clearly as well as the position different groups took. There is a knockout hook that includes one of the most famous leads taken from the bible story of Genesis, which heightens the reader's interest.

**Target Area 2: Continuity**—If you have continuity in your writing, you make uninterrupted connections.

A good piece of writing moves along smoothly like a champion figure skater making a figure eight. There are no sudden stops and starts, no stumbling, no bumpiness. Each paragraph flows from one to the next. There is **continuity**; the sentences are clearly connected moving toward and supporting one central idea or focus.

When you write an essay with continuity, you are continually making uninterrupted connections with all of your paragraphs to your central idea known as the thesis. This is perfected by beginning with a topic sentence and ending with a concluding sentence.

Read the following paragraph that would typically be written by a student answering this document-based task question, **How did the environment affect the lives of Native Americans?**

*Writer's first paragraph:*

The pre-Columbian period had many people move to Alaska. These people were called Native Americans. The environment affected their lives by the tools they used. They were affected by the animals they hunted. They were affected by the climate and geography in which they lived.

*Topic Sentence for Second Paragraph:*
A tool the Makah used was a harpoon.

**Now read the writer's revision for continuity.** Read the same paragraph with a few strategically placed words in boldface. Notice how the writer establishes continuity from the beginning of the essay. The last sentence of the beginning paragraph is picked up and carried forward by the beginning sentence of the second paragraph.

*Writer's revised first paragraph:*
**During** the pre-Columbian period, many people migrated across a huge land bridge that connected Asia with Alaska. **These** people, who scientists call the first Native Americans, followed the Ice Age mammals into the Americas. The environment affected their lives in several important ways: the tools they used, the food they ate, and the climate and geography in which they lived.

*Writer's revised topic sentence for second paragraph:*
**Because** of the abundance of large water life in a cool climate, the Makah, a Native American group of the Northwest, invented a specialized tool for hunting called the harpoon.

A word, a phrase, and sometimes a whole sentence in one paragraph directs the mind of the reader to go back very briefly to what was said and then forward to what is about to be said. The writer skillfully revises using the transition words *during, these,* and *because.* These expressions are called transitions because they bridge the gap between sentences and paragraphs. In Chapter 6, you will find a chart of common transitions used in good writing. Study their meanings and usages, and practice using them in all parts of your document-based essay.

As you can see, when you connect ideas from one paragraph to the next, it is important that you repeat an important word or phrase used in the previous paragraph. You can achieve continuity when you frequently refer to the thesis of the essay.

You will achieve continuity in your paragraphs if you begin all paragraphs with a topic sentence that is linked by a transitional word or phrase from the preceding paragraphs.

Look at the following paragraph and related first line or topic sentence of the second paragraph. Identify the transition and the repeated idea.

The environment greatly impacted the lives of pre-Columbian Native Americans. The climate and geography affected the type of tools that were created, the type and amount of food consumed, and their dwelling places.

One pre-Columbian Native American group, the Makah of Alaska, used special tools to hunt sea and land mammals.

In paragraph one, the thesis, "The environment greatly impacted the lives of the Native Americans," is clearly stated in line one. The second line develops this thesis by stating two aspects of the environment: **climate** and **geography.** It also gives three specific examples of how the environment affects people: **tools, food, and dwelling places.** The topic sentence of the second paragraph includes the transitional phrase: "One pre-Columbian Native American group" and repeats the keyword "tools."

**Target Area 3—Redundancy**—As a good writer, you should avoid pointless repetition.

Reading your writing to yourself as you write will help you avoid repeating unnecessary words or phrases. The key word is **unnecessary**. Sometimes it is necessary to repeat words and ideas especially when connecting your introduction to your conclusion. Perhaps you want to link one idea from one paragraph to another paragraph. In that case, you will repeat a phrase. Just make sure that you are deleting information that is already said and explained. When it is not necessary to repeat it for the reader's understanding, it's best to leave it out.

The usual repetition in most students' writing happens when a thesis statement with examples and details (specificity) is not developed completely. Instead the writer says the same thing over and over again to fill up space. This should be avoided.

Examine the paragraph below. Can you tell which words are unnecessarily repeated?

The Underground Railroad was a big help to slaves that were escaping. There is a picture of people taking the Underground Railroad route to escape from slavery. The Underground Railroad was a secret group of people who helped slaves escape.

Now, look at the **revised** paragraph. The repeated information is eliminated. Details and examples have been added to make the writing meaningful and to develop and support the thesis.

Some abolitionists—people who opposed slavery—were willing to risk their lives to help African Americans escape from slavery. They organized the Underground Railroad, which was a secret network of escape routes that provided protection and transportation for runaway slaves who wanted to reach freedom in the North and Canada.

**Target Area 4—Introductions and Conclusions**—Connect them.

Make sure you have developed your introduction with specificity from the historical context and the task question. Write an interesting hook. This should enable you to develop four to six sentences in your beginning paragraph that does four things:

1. Get the reader's attention
2. Clearly state what you will prove.
3. Give your opinion.
4. Lead into the next paragraph with appropriate transitions.

Your conclusion should restate your thesis. (To restate means to use similar but slightly different words.) It should contain appropriate concluding transitions, and remind the reader of the general points made in the entire essay while also leaving the reader with a lasting impression.

**Target Area 5—Vital Verbs**—History is the past, so use the past tense.

1. Examine the incorrect verb tense of **write,** before revision.

   In order to improve the original document, the founding fathers write many amendments to the Constitution.

   After revision:

   In order to improve the original document, the founding fathers **wrote** many amendments to the Constitution.

2. Use **strong** verbs, and although it's not always possible, try to avoid forms of the verb **to be** when you can: **is, am, are, was, were, be, been, being.**

3. Revise for troublesome verbs: **Lie, lay, bring, brought.** Examine the verb **lie** in the sentence below. The verb **lie** means to **rest** or **recline.**

   The Union army was badly scattered and the men were tired. They needed to **lie** down and rest in order to regain their strength.

4. Examine the past tense of the verb to **lie,** which is **lay** in the sentence below.

   The men were allowed to **lie** down and rest for several hours.

5. Examine the verb **bring** in the sentence below. The word **bring** means **to carry.**

   The messenger did not **bring** the secret message in time to notify the Union army about the impending raid. By nightfall, the Confederate army surprised the troops.

6. Examine the past tense of **bring** which is **brought** in the sentence below.

   The message was not **brought** to the Union army as planned. Instead, the Confederate army intercepted the message and held the messenger prisoner.

**Target Area 6—Sentence Combining**—Combine two sentences into one using **and** or **but.**

Change the period at the end of the first sentence to a comma. Add the word **but**—to show a contrast and to show additional information.

**1.** Examine these two sentences below before revision.

The greatest number of enslaved Africans worked on farms and plantations in the South.

Slavery existed to some extent in all the American colonies.

Now examine how these two sentences can be combined with the word **but** after revision.

The greatest number of enslaved Africans worked on farms and plantations in the South, **but** slavery existed to some extent in each of the American colonies.

**2.** Examine these two sentences below before revision.

The English government had to raise money to pay a debt.

The English government had to support thousands of British troops who had been sent to patrol America's wilderness frontier.

Now, examine how these sentences can be combined using the word **and** after revision.

The English government had to raise money to pay a debt, **and** had to support thousands of troops who had been sent to patrol America's wilderness frontier.

**3.** Sentence combining using **who** and **which**. The word **who** is used to refer to a person. Examine these two sentences before revision.

Harriet Tubman was an escaped slave.

Harriet Tubman founded the Underground Railroad.

Now, examine the sentences combined using the word **who** after revision.

Harriet Tubman, **who** was an escaped slave, founded the Underground Railroad.

**4.** Examine the sentences below before revision.

Runaway slaves were treated harshly when captured.

The Fugitive Slave Law made runaway slaves in the north illegal.

And after revision:

The Fugitive Slave Law made runaway slaves, who were treated harshly when captured, illegal in the north.

**5.** Examine the sentences below before revision.

President Abraham Lincoln wrote the Emancipation Proclamation.

The Emancipation Proclamation declared that all slaves were free.

After revision:

President Abraham Lincoln wrote the Emancipation Proclamation that declared all slaves were free.

In order to combine short, related sentences it is also useful to remember these special combining words: *after, although, when, which, while, how, if, that, even though, because, before, unless, until, since, and so that.* Knowing these words will also give you the power to revise sentence fragments (incomplete sentences).

**6.** Examine this fragment and complete sentence before revision.

When the southern states seceded from the Union.

They were protesting the antislavery position of the north.

Now, examine the combined fragment and sentence that uses the combining word *when.*

**When** the southern states seceded from the Union, they were protesting the antislavery position of the North.

It's time to put these revision strategies to actual use in a sample document-based essay that includes historical background, a task question, and primary source documents.

The following is a typical example of a document-based question about the Civil War.

**Historical Context:** During the first half of the nineteenth century, the spirit of manifest destiny led to a substantial increase in the geographic size of the United States. As territories were settled and new states were formed, the issue of the spread of slavery divided the nation. While some Americans worked tirelessly to abolish slavery, others stood firm in the belief that the right to own a slave should not be decided by the federal government.

Task: Review all of the following documents and answer the corresponding questions. Based upon your knowledge of social studies and the documents, write a well-developed essay in which you answer this question:

What was the impact of slavery on people from all regions of the United States?

---

## Key Vocabulary

**abolitionists:** people who wanted to end slavery in the United States

**civil war:** war between people of the same country

**compromise:** settlement in which each side gives up some of its demands in order to reach an agreement

**Emancipation Proclamation:** President Lincoln's declaration freeing the slaves in the Confederacy

**fugitive slave:** runaway slave

**Gettysburg Address:** speech by President Lincoln after the Battle of Gettysburg

**plantations:** large estate farmed by many workers

**popular sovereignty:** idea that the people hold the final authority in government, allowing each territory to decide whether to allow slavery

**sectionalism:** loyalty to a state or section rather than to the whole country

**states' rights:** idea that states have the right to limit the power of the federal government

---

These are the documents to which the student referred:

## DOCUMENT 1

### *Calhoun's Views of Slavery, His Character, His Personality by John S. Jenkins 1850*

Calhoun believed that slavery was a political tradition that was in use before the U.S. government was formed and documented in the Constitution. The creators of the Constitution viewed slaves as property rather than citizens, and supported the right to own slaves. Calhoun supported the right for slave owners in areas not omitted by the Missouri Compromise to be protected in that right to own slaves in other states in addition to the slave states.

In addition, Calhoun believed that slavery in the South was productive. He stated that the Negro race reached a high level of morals, intelligence, and civilization that had not been reached anywhere or anytime before. He claimed that slavery existed in all civilized countries. He questioned the correctness of this phrase from the Declaration of Independence that all men are born free and equal. Also, he states that natural rights in every age in every country are controlled by political institutions. Calhoun believed that colored people were a substandard race and that slavery was not a humiliation. On the contrary, he stated that slavery, in fact, had a positive effect and tended to improve the social, moral, and intellectual condition of slaves. He goes on to say that the southern slaves' situation was enviable compared to the free slaves in the north or with the working classes in England. The Negro slave, he claimed, knew his inferiority, and believed his position as a slave was proper. The two races cannot exist equally in a country where the numbers are the same. One must be subjugated to the other. He believed that abolitionists were jeopardizing the happiness and peace of the Union.

*Source*: HistoryCentral.com

**Summary of John Jenkins article about Calhoun's views on slavery:** In the above document, John Jenkins summarizes the views of John C. Calhoun, a respected Southern senator of the 1800s. The question of slavery caused great conflict in our nation in the 1800s. The debate about which of the newly acquired western lands should be slave-free became a national crisis. Calhoun opposed a plan proposed by Henry Clay, a respected senator from Kentucky, known as the Compromise of 1850. This compromise also attempted to keep the balance between slave and free states so that neither would have more power in the Senate. Calhoun spoke against these lands becoming slave-free. Jenkins summarizes Calhoun's view that reflected the white southern plantation owners' view of slavery. Calhoun believed that the Negro race was inferior to whites. Also, he believed that black slaves were better off as slaves and that their slavery actually improved their race. In his view, the federal government had no business denying the rights of its citizens to bring property to the new lands. To the southerners, slaves were their property, and they believed that the federal government should have protected their right to own slaves.

*Source:* HistoryCentral.com

## DOCUMENT 2

### *Lecompton Constitution—1857*
### *Article VII*
### *Slavery*

Section 1. The right of property is more important than any constitutional allowance (authorization). The right of a slave owner to own slaves is the same unbreakable right as any U.S. citizen to own property.

Section 2. The legislature does not have the power to pass laws to free slaves without the permission of the slave owners, or without paying the owners before slaves are set free. Also, the legislature has no power to stop citizens who enter different states from bringing slaves with them. The legislature may write laws that stop slaves who have committed serious crimes from entering a new state or territory. They have the power to pass laws to allow the owners of slaves to free them. They shall have the power to make sure that the owners of slaves treat them with kindness, to provide for them necessary food and clothing, to refrain from all injuries to them extending to life or limb, and, in case of their neglect or refusal to go along with the direction of such laws, to have such slave or slaves sold for the benefit of the owner or owners.

Section 3. In the prosecution of slaves for crimes of higher grade than petit larceny, the legislature shall have no power to deprive them of an impartial trial by a petit jury.

Section 4. Any person who shall maliciously dismember or deprive a slave of life shall suffer such punishment as would be indicted in case the like offense had been committed on a free white person, and on the like proof, except in case of insurrection of such slave.

Section 7. This constitution shall be given to the Congress of the United States at its next session . . . Before this constitution shall be given to Congress, it shall be given to all the white male inhabitants of this Territory, for approval or disapproval, as follows: . . . The voting shall be by ballot. The ballots will be cast for either Constitution with slavery and Constitution with no slavery. If the majority of votes cast are in favor of Constitution with no slavery then slavery shall no longer exist in Kansas, except that the right of property in slaves not in this Territory shall in no manner be interfered with.

*Source*: HistoryCentral.com

**Summary of LeCompton Constitution:** In 1857, a small proslavery group in Kansas sent elected members to a convention in order to write their own constitution. A constitution was required in order to gain statehood. The result was a proslavery document called the LeCompton Constitution. Most Kansans were opposed to slavery and refused to vote on the constitution. When Congress returned the constitution to Kansas for another vote, it was defeated.

*Source*: HistoryCentral.com

## DOCUMENT 3

### *Emancipation Proclamation*

January 1, 1863

Where, on . . . [September 22, 1862] . . . , a proclamation was given by the President of the United States, containing among other things, the following, to wit:

"That on . . . [January 1, 1863] . . . , all persons held as slaves within any state or designated part of a state, the people there shall then be in rebellion against the United States, shall be then, from this time on, and forever, free; and the Executive Government of the United States, including the military and naval authority, will recognize and maintain the freedom of people, and will do no act or acts to stop people, in any effort they may make to be free.

"That the Executive will, on the first day of January as stated before by proclamation, designate the states and parts of the states, if any, in which people shall then be in rebellion against the United States; and the fact that any state, or the people in that state, shall on that day be in good faith represented in the Congress of the United States, by members chosen at elections where a majority of the voters of such states shall have participated, shall, in the absence of strong countervailing testimony, be deemed conclusive evidence that such state, and the people in it, are not then in rebellion against the United States."

Now, therefore, I, ABRAHAM LINCOLN, President of the United States, by virtue of the power in me vested as commander-in-chief of the army and navy of the United States, in time of actual armed rebellion against the authority and Government of the United States, and as a fit and necessary war measure for stopping said rebellion, do, on this first day of January, . . . [1863], and in accordance with my purpose so to do, publicly proclaimed for the full period of one hundred days from the day first above mentioned, order and designate as the states and parts of states wherein the people thereof, respectively, are this day in rebellion against the United States, the following, to wit: Arkansas, Texas, Louisiana, (except the parishes of St. Bernard, Plaquemines, Jefferson, St. John, St. Charles, St. James, Ascension, Assumption, Terre Bonne, Lafourche, St. Mary, St. Martin, and Orleans, including the city of New Orleans,) Mississippi, Alabama, Florida, Georgia, South Carolina, North Carolina, and Virginia, (except the forty-eight counties designated as West Virginia, and also the counties of Berkeley, Accomac, Northampton, Elizabeth City, York, Princess Ann, and Norfolk, including the cities of Norfolk and Portsmouth,) and which excepted parts are for the present left precisely as if this proclamation were not issued.

And by virtue of the power and for the purpose aforesaid, I do order and declare that all people help as slaves within said designated states and parts of states are, and henceforward shall be, free; and that the Executive Government of the United States, including the military and naval authorities thereof, will recognize and maintain the freedom of said persons.

And I hereby enjoin upon the people so declared to be free to abstain from all violence, unless in necessary self-defense; and I recommend to them that, in all cases when allowed, they labor faithfully for reasonable wages.

And I further declare and make known that such persons, of suitable condition, will be received into the armed service of the United States to garrison forts, positions, stations, and other places, and to man vessels of all sorts in said service.

And upon this act, sincerely believed to be an act of justice, warranted by the Constitution upon military necessity, I invoke the considerate judgment of mankind and the gracious favor of Almighty God.

*Source:* HistoryCentral.com

**Summary of the Emancipation Proclamation:** On New Year's Day, 1863, slaves in areas of rebellion against the government would be free. This meant that only certain slaves were considered free: those living under Confederate control. Slaves in the border states and living in Confederate areas under Union control were not freed. This document did not bring about an immediate end to slavery. However, it inspired southern slaves who heard about it and encouraged them to escape to the Union army, which many did join.

*Source:* HistoryCentral.com

## DOCUMENT 4

### *Clay's Resolutions*

January 29, 1850
It being desirable, for the peace, concord, and harmony of the Union of these States, to settle and adjust amicably all existing questions of controversy between them arising out of the institution of slavery upon a fair, equitable and just basis: therefore,

1. Resolved, That California, with suitable boundaries, ought, upon her application to be admitted as one of trio States of this Union, without the imposition by Congress of any restriction in respect to the exclusion or introduction of slavery within those boundaries.

2. Resolved, That as slavery does not exist by law, and is not likely to be introduced into any of the territory acquired by the United States from the republic of Mexico, it is inexpedient for Congress to provide by law either for its introduction into, or exclusion from, any part of the said territory; and that appropriate territorial governments ought to be established by Congress in all of the said territory, not assigned as the boundaries of the proposed State of California, without the adoption of any restriction or condition on the subject of slavery.

3. Resolved, That the western boundary of the State of Texas ought to be fixed on the Rio del Norte, commencing one marine league from its mouth, and running up that river to the southern line of New Mexico; thence with that line eastwardly, and so continuing in the same direction to the line as established between the United States and Spain, excluding any portion of New Mexico, whether lying on the east or west of that river.

5. Resolved, That it be proposed to the State of Texas, that the United States will provide for the payment of all that portion of the legitimate and bona fide public debt of that State contracted prior to its annexation to the United States, and for which the duties on foreign imports were pledged by the said State to its creditors, not exceeding the sum of dollars, in consideration of the said duties so pledged having been no longer applicable to that object after the said annexation, but having thenceforward become payable to the United States; and upon the condition, also, that the said State of Texas shall, by some solemn and authentic act of her legislature or of a convention; relinquish to the United States any claim which it has to any part of New Mexico.

6. Resolved, That it is inexpedient to abolish slavery in the District of Columbia whilst that institution continues to exist in the State of Maryland, without the consent of that State, without the consent of the people of the District, and without just compensation to the owners of slaves within the District.

7. But, resolved, That it is expedient to prohibit, within the District, the slave trade in slaves brought into it from States or places beyond the limits of the District, either to be sold therein as merchandise, or to be transported to other markets without the District of Columbia.

8. Resolved, That more effectual provision ought to be made by law, according to the requirement of the constitution, for the restitution and delivery of persons bound to service or labor in any State, who may escape into any other State or Territory in the Union. And,

9. Resolved, That Congress has no power to prohibit or obstruct the trade in slaves between the slaveholding States; but that the admission or exclusion of slaves brought from one into another of them, depends exclusively upon their own particular laws.

*Source:* HistoryCentral.com

**Summary of Clay's Resolutions:** In order to help ease tensions between the North and the South over the issue of slavery, Henry Clay, a respected Senator from Kentucky, tried to solve the slavery debate peacefully by proposing laws that favored both the North and the South. Northerners opposed the spread of slavery in newly acquired lands. For the North, Clay's proposal stated California would be admitted to the Union as a free state, no slaves. The second law supported popular sovereignty, whereby the people of New Mexico and Utah would decide if slavery would be legal. Also, the selling of slaves would end in Washington, D.C. For the South, slavery would remain legal. In addition, the Fugitive Slave Act would make it difficult for slaves to escape to the North because it required northerners to help catch runaway slaves.

*Source:* HistoryCentral.com

## DOCUMENT 5

## *Fugitive Slave Act*

September 18, 1850

An Act to amend, and supplementary to, the Act entitled "An Act respecting Fugitives from Justice, and Persons escaping from the service of their Masters," approved . . . [February 12, 1793].

[Sections 1–4 relate to the appointment of commissioners, having concurrent jurisdiction with the judges of the circuit and district courts of the United States, and the superior courts of the territories, to perform the duties specified in the act.]

**SEC. 5.** And be it further enacted, That it shall be the duty of all marshals and deputy marshals to obey and execute all warrants and precepts issued under the provisions of this act, when to them directed; and should any marshal or deputy marshal refuse to receive such warrant, or other process, when tendered, or to use all proper means diligently to execute the same, he shall, on conviction thereof, be fined in the sum of one thousand dollars, to the use of such claimant, on the motion of such claimant, by the Circuit or District Court for the district of such marshal; and after arrest of such fugitive, by such marshal or his deputy, or whilst at any time in his custody under the provisions of this act, should such fugitive escape, whether with or without the assent of such marshal or his deputy, such marshal shall be liable, on his official bond, to be prosecuted for the benefit of such claimant, for the full value of the service or labor of said fugitive in the State, Territory, or District whence he escaped: and the better to enable the said commissioners, when thus appointed, to execute their duties faithfully and efficiently, in conformity with the requirements of the Constitution of the United States and of this act, they are hereby authorized and empowered, within their counties respectively, to appoint, in writing under their hands, any one or more suitable persons, from time to time, to execute all such warrants and other process as may be issued by them in the lawful performance of their respective duties; with authority to such commissioners, or the persons to be appointed by them, to execute process as aforesaid, to summon and call to their aid the bystanders, or posse comitatus of the proper county, when necessary to ensure a faithful observance of the clause of the Constitution referred to, in conformity with the provisions of this act; and all good citizens are hereby commanded to aid and assist in the prompt and efficient execution of this law, whenever their services may be required, as aforesaid, for that purpose; and said warrants shall run, and be executed by said officers, any where in the State within which they are issued.

**SEC. 6.** And be it further enacted, That when a person held to service or labor in any State or Territory of the United States, has heretofore or shall hereafter escape into another State or Territory of the United States, the person or persons to whom such service or labor may be due, or his, her, or their agent or attorney, duly authorized, by power of attorney, in writing, . . . may pursue and reclaim such fugitive person, either by procuring a warrant from some one of the courts, judges, or commissioners aforesaid, of the proper circuit, district, or county, for the apprehension of such fugitive from service or labor, or by seizing and arresting such fugitive, where the same can be done without process, and by taking, or causing such person to be taken, forthwith before such court, judge, or commissioner, whose duty it shall be to hear and determine the case of such claimant in a summary manner; and upon satisfactory proof being made, by deposition or affidavit, in writing, to be taken and certified by such court, judge, or commissioner, or by other satisfactory testimony, duly taken and certified by some court, magistrate, justice of the peace, or other legal officer authorized to administer an oath and take depositions under the laws of the State or Territory from which such person owing service or labor may have escaped, with a certificate of such magistracy or other authority, as aforesaid, . . . and with proof, also by affidavit, of the identity of the person whose service or labor is claimed to be due as aforesaid, that the person so arrested does in fact owe service or labor to the person or persons claiming him or her, in the State or Territory from which such fugitive may have escaped as aforesaid, and that said person escaped, to make out and deliver to such claimant, his or her agent or attorney, a certificate setting forth the substantial facts as to the service or labor due from such fugitive to the claimant, and of his or her escape from the State or Territory in which he or she was arrested, with authority to such claimant, or his or her agent or attorney, to use such reasonable force and restraint as may be necessary, under the circumstances of the case, to take and remove such fugitive person back to the State or Territory whence he or she may have escaped as aforesaid. In no trial or hearing under this act shall the testimony of such alleged fugitive be admitted in evidence; and the certificates in this and the first [fourth] section mentioned, shall be conclusive of the right of the person or persons in whose favor granted, to remove such fugitive to the State or Territory from which he escaped, and shall prevent all molestation of such person or persons by any process issued by any court, judge, magistrate, or other person whomsoever.

SEC. 7. And be it further enacted, That any person who shall knowingly and willingly obstruct, hinder, or prevent such claimant, his agent or attorney, or any person or persons lawfully assisting him, her, or them, from arresting such a fugitive from service or labor, either with or without process as aforesaid, or shall rescue, or attempt to rescue, such fugitive from service or labor, from the custody of such claimant, his or her agent or attorney, or other person or persons lawfully assisting as aforesaid, when so arrested, pursuant to the authority herein given and declared; or shall aid, abet, or assist such person so owing service or labor as aforesaid, directly or indirectly, to escape from such claimant, his agent or attorney, or other person or persons legally authorized as aforesaid; or shall harbor or conceal such fugitive, so as to prevent the discovery and arrest of such person, after notice or knowledge of the fact that such person was a fugitive from service or labor as aforesaid, shall, for either of said offenses, be subject to a fine not exceeding one thousand dollars, and imprisonment not exceeding six months . . . ; and shall moreover forfeit and pay, by way of civil damages to the party injured by such illegal conduct, the sum of one thousand dollars, for each fugitive so lost as aforesaid . . .

SEC. 9. And be it further enacted, That, upon affidavit made by the claimant of such fugitive, his agent or attorney, after such certificate has been issued, that he has reason to apprehend that such fugitive will be rescued by force from his or their possession before he can be taken beyond the limits of the State in which the arrest is made, it shall be the duty of the officer making the arrest to retain such fugitive in his custody, and to remove him to the State whence he fled, and there to deliver him to said claimant, his agent, or attorney. And to this end, the officer aforesaid is hereby authorized and required to employ so many persons as he may deem necessary to overcome such force, and to retain them in his service so long as circumstances may require. . . .

SEC. 10. And be it further enacted, That when any person held to service or labor in any State or Territory, or in the District of Columbia, shall escape there from, the party to whom such service or labor shall be due, his, her, or their agent or attorney, may apply to any court of record therein, or judge thereof in vacation, and make satisfactory proof to such court, or judge in vacation, of the escape aforesaid, and that the person escaping owed service or labor to such party. Whereupon the court shall cause a record to be made of the matters so proved, and also a general description of the person so escaping, with such convenient certainty as may be; and a transcript of such record, authenticated by the attestation of the clerk and of the seal of the said court, being produced in any other State, Territory, or district in which the person so escaping may be found, and being exhibited to any judge, commissioner, or other officer authorized by the law of the United States to cause persons escaping from service or labor to be delivered up, shall be held and taken to be full and conclusive evidence of the fact of escape, and that the service or labor of the person escaping is due to the party in such record mentioned. And upon the production by the said party of other and further evidence if necessary, either oral or by affidavit, in addition to what is contained in the said record of the identity of the person escaping, he or she shall be delivered up to the claimant. And the said court, commissioner, judge, or other person authorized by this act to grant certificates to claimants of fugitives, shall, upon the production of the record and other evidences aforesaid, grant to such claimant a certificate of his right to take any such person identified and proved to be owing service or labor as aforesaid, which certificate shall authorize such claimant to seize or arrest and transport such person to the State or Territory from which he escaped . . .

*Source:* HistoryCentral.com

**Summary of the Fugitive Slave Act:** This law was part of the Compromise of 1850 that ordered all citizens of the United States to help return all escaped slaves to their owners. It also denied a jury trial to escaped slaves.

*Source:* HistoryCentral.com

## DOCUMENT 6

### *Address at Gettysburg, Pennsylvania—November 19, 1863*
### *(Delivered at the dedication of the Cemetery at Gettysburg.)*

Four score and seven years ago our fathers brought forth on this continent, a new nation, conceived in Liberty, and dedicated to the proposition that all men are created equal. Now we are engaged in a great civil war, testing whether that nation or any nation so conceived and so dedicated, can long endure. We are met on a great battlefield of that war. We have come to dedicate a portion of that field, as a final resting place for those who here gave their lives that that nation might live. It is altogether fitting and proper that we should do this. But, in a larger sense, we cannot dedicate, we cannot consecrate—we cannot hallow this ground. The brave men, living and dead, who struggled here, have consecrated it, far above our poor power to add or detract. The world will little note, nor long remember what we say here, but it can never forget what they did here. It is for us the living, rather, to be dedicated here to the unfinished work which they who fought here have thus far so nobly advanced. It is rather for us to be here dedicated to the great task remaining before us— that from these honored dead we take increased devotion to that cause for which they gave the last full measure of devotion—that we here highly resolve that these dead shall not have died in vain—that this nation, under God, shall have a new birth of freedom and that government of the people, by the people, for the people, shall not perish from the earth.

*Source:* HistoryCentral.com

**Summary of The Gettysburg Address:** On November 19, 1863, a dedication ceremony was held at a Gettysburg cemetery to honor the Union soldiers who had died there. President Abraham Lincoln's brief speech supported the principles of freedom and equality for all Americans. He said that the living must go on and finish the work for which the soldiers had died. The Union must protect the freedom of all its people.

*Source*: HistoryCentral.com

## DOCUMENT 7

## *Amendment 5*

No person shall be held to answer for a **capital,** or otherwise **infamous** crime, unless on a presentment or **indictment** of a grand jury, except in cases arising in the land or naval forces, or in the militia, when in actual service in time of war or public danger; nor shall any person be subject for the same offense to be twice put in **jeopardy** of life and limb; nor shall be **compelled,** in any criminal case, to be a witness against himself; nor be **deprived** of life, liberty or property, without **due process** of law; nor shall private property be taken for public use, without just **compensation.**

---

### Key Vocabulary

**capital crime:** a crime punishable by death

**infamous:** notoriously bad

**indictment:** accusation

**jeopardy:** danger

**compelled:** forced

**deprived:** denied

**due process:** fair trial

**compensation:** payment

---

## DOCUMENT 8

## *Amendment 10*

The powers not **delegated** to the United States by the Constitution, nor **prohibited** by it to the states, are **reserved** to the states respectively, or to the people.

## Key Vocabulary

**delegated:** given out

**prohibited:** stopped

**reserved:** set aside

Let's take a close look at a typical student essay answer to the above document-based question with an evaluator's commentary and revision.

**Task Question:** What was the impact of slavery on people from all regions of the United States?

### First Draft

During the first half of the nineteenth century, the spirit of **Manifest Destiny** is important to the United States. **Manifest destiny** led to an increase in the geographic size of the United States. As time went on territories were settled and new states were formed. The spread of slavery divided the nation. While some people tried very hard to abolish slavery, others fought for the right of people to own a slave. They believe this issue should not be decided by the federal government, but rather by individual states. The slavery issue led to the debate over states' rights and impacted all regions of the United States. The Fugitive Slave Law, the Lecompton Constitution of Kansas, the Underground Railroad, the Emancipation Proclamation, and the Gettysburg address all had a profound impact on the lives of American citizens.

Henry Clay created resolutions in order to create peace, concord, and harmony in the United States. He wanted to peacefully settle all questions about the slavery controversy. He wanted California admitted into the Union with no conditions regarding slavery and he created a tough fugitive slave law for runaway slaves.

Slaves lived with different degrees of deprivation and punishment. All slaves had one thing in common: no liberty. It was no surprise that many would escape using the Underground Railroad. The Underground Railroad was a big help to escaped slaves. The Underground Railroad was a path with a series of hiding places to help people go through it. And the person who helped them to go through it was a woman named Harriet Tubman. The railroad is not a real railroad; it is a place where slaves traveled to gain freedom. They wanted to get to freedom in the north. The interpretation of U.S. Constitutional Amendments Five and Ten had a major impact on the plight of slaves. Slavery supporters interpreted Amendment Five as guaranteeing slavery.

In President Lincoln's Gettysburg Address of November 1863, he redefined the United States by restating what was meant by "all men are created equal." This phrase from the Declaration of Independence did not include African Americans. Although the founding fathers meant this protection for a few privileged white men only, Lincoln clearly means all people, regardless of race. Lincoln's words have had a great impact on how our country defines freedom. This speech paved the way for all American citizens to have the guarantee of freedom and equality. His speech clearly put all supporters of slavery at odds with the United States government.

In conclusion, the reader can see how the issue of slavery impacted all regions of the United States. It was a tense time in the history of the United States.

## The Reviewer's Comments:

*Evaluation of introduction:*

- This essay has unnecessary repetition. For writing that is more concise, the first two sentences should be combined. This eliminates redundancy from the essay.
- This paragraph lacks specificity. Manifest Destiny should be defined more clearly.
- There is no clear thesis for this essay. Although some of the historical background is given and the writer touches on important effects of slavery, the impact of slavery is not clearly explained.
- An incorrect verb tense is used throughout the essay. For example: "Manifest Destiny is . . ." "They believe . . ." Since the events took place in the past, it is best to use the past tense.

*Evaluation of body paragraphs:*

- This essay lacks a transitional sentence to connect the second paragraph to the thesis.
- The introduction of this essay lacks specificity. By asking the questions: "Who is Henry Clay?" or "What impact did the interpretation of constitutional Amendments Five and Ten have on slavery?" the writer could have added more details.
- The writer could have elaborated and explained the effects of the resolution and its link to the slavery debate in order to make a point.
- The body of the essay lacks continuity. No transitional link can be found between paragraphs two and three.
- Although documents are introduced in the introduction, some are not mentioned or elaborated in the body of the essay.
- The body of the essay is also weak because it repeats information. Terms and phrases about the Underground Railroad are mentioned again and again. Sentence combining would be an effective technique to use here.
- The writer uses an incorrect verb tense: "Lincoln clearly means . . ."

*Evaluation of Conclusion:*

- To be more effective, the last paragraph should restate the thesis.
- Using specific details would make the essay more effective.
- For clarity, major points should be elaborated and explained.

This essay would not get the best grade. Now take a look at a draft that has been revised.

**Task Question:** What was the impact of slavery on people from all regions of the United States?

### Revised Draft:

In the first half of the nineteenth century, the new nation of America grappled with this debate: Was slavery acceptable, a popular sentiment among supporters of slavery, or detestable, as it was to abolitionists? Simultaneously, the spirit of Manifest Destiny—the philosophy that Americans have a right and duty to expand our territories West to the far reaches of the Pacific Ocean—led to an increase in the geographic size of the United States. As time went on, territories settled in new states that were formed. While various individuals, groups, politicians, and statesmen tried to decide which territories should or should not be slave-free, the spread of slavery divided the nation. While some people tried very hard to abolish slavery, others fought for the right of people to own slaves. They believed this issue should not be decided by the federal government, but rather by individual states. The slavery issue led to the debate over states' rights and impacted all regions of the United States. The resulting debate led to many conflicting laws, declarations, and decisions such as the Fugitive Slave Law, the Lecompton Constitution of Kansas, the Dred Scott Decision, the Underground Railroad, the Emancipation Proclamation, and the Gettysburg Address, all of which had a profound impact on the lives of American citizens from each section of the United States. **The issue of African American enslavement more than any other issue was at the heart of the philosophical and economic controversy that dominated the political and social tensions of all sections of the United States leading up to the Civil War.**

While the North based its economy mostly on industry and paid workers, southerners supported slavery because their economy depended on slave labor. Large and small plantations were prospering due to the production of cotton. Slave owners believed that slaves were their property. Senator John C. Calhoun from South Carolina represented the southern position. He argued that the newly formed western territories were not the property of the federal government, but rather of all the states together. He debated that Congress had no right to prohibit any type of property in these territories, by which he meant slaves, that was legal in any of the states. Calhoun and supporters of slavery interpreted the Fifth and Tenth Amendments of the Constitution as supporting each state's right to be a slave state or a free state. In their minds, slaves were property that was guaranteed in Amendment Five of the Constitution that states that no one can be "deprived of life, liberty, or property, without due process of law." Differing economies and interpretation of laws divided the North and South in their views of slave labor.

To ease tensions between southerners and northerners, Henry Clay proposed a compromise. In this compromise, known as the Compromise of 1850, California would be a free state, the New Mexico and Utah Territories would not be specifically reserved for slavery, but would be decided by popular sovereignty, and the slave trade would be abolished in the District of Columbia. In return, the South received a tough Fugitive Slave Law. The law enraged Northerners, many of whom believed it essentially legalized kidnapping. Under its provisions, African Americans living in the North and claimed by slave catchers were denied trial by jury and many of the protections of due process. The law required that all U.S. citizens aid in the capture and return of fugitives. Although Clay wanted to settle all questions about the slavery controversy peacefully, the impact of this law polarized the country even further.

Politicians hoped that the Supreme Court would settle the slavery controversy after it heard the case of *Dred Scott v. Sanford*. This case involved a Missouri slave, Dred Scott, who had been encouraged by abolitionists to sue for his freedom on the basis that his owner, an army doctor, had taken him for a stay of several years in a free state, Illinois, and then in a free territory, Wisconsin. The court ruled that Scott had no standing to sue in federal court, and that temporary residence in a free state, even for several years, did not make a slave free, and that the Missouri Compromise was unconstitutional because Congress did not have the authority to exclude slavery from any territory. Instead of settling the sectional controversy, this decision made it worse.

While many southern whites were working hard to spread slavery, many African Americans and their sympathizers were also hard at work trying to stop slavery altogether. The pro-slavery government of Kansas created a pro-slavery constitution that would allow slavery if Kansas became a state. Kansas's voters turned down the Lecompton Constitution, choosing to remain a territory rather than become a slave state. Although slaves lived with different degrees of deprivation and punishment, all had one thing in common: no liberty. It was no surprise that many would escape using the Underground Railroad. This extraordinary "railroad" was a relay system of abolitionists who helped runaway slaves reach freedom in the North and Canada. Its most famous conductor was Harriet Tubman, herself an escaped slave. The antislavery movement gained even more momentum with the publishing of Harriet Beecher Stowe's *Uncle Tom's Cabin*, which graphically depicts the immoral effects of slavery.

The impact of slavery made its way to the President of the United States. In January 1863, Lincoln proclaimed that all people held as slaves were free in those states in rebellion that have left the Union. In President Lincoln's Gettysburg Address of November 1863, he redefined the United States by restating what was meant by "all men are created equal." This phrase from the Declaration of Independence did not originally include African Americans. Although the founding fathers intended this protection for a few privileged white men only, Lincoln clearly meant all people, regardless of race. Lincoln's words have had a great impact on how our country defines freedom. This speech paved the way for all American citizens to have the guarantee of freedom and equality. His speech put all supporters of slavery at odds with the U.S. government.

The issue of African American enslavement had a profound impact on the lives of all Americans in the Civil War era. As Lincoln said in his acceptance speech for the Illinois senate, "A house divided against itself cannot stand. I believe this government cannot endure permanently half slave and half free." The debate became not only a question of economics and politics, but also a moral issue. According to Paul Robeson, "If Negro freedom is taken away, or that of any minority group, the freedom of all the people is taken away." American citizens and leaders should never lose sight of how much turmoil, pain, and bloodshed our country experienced, and should be ever vigilant in protecting the ideal set forth in the Declaration of Independence and further explained in the United States Constitution that "all men are created equal."

The writer used this simple checklist to revise the essays and to get a better grade.

*Revision Checklist:*
- ✔ Do I have a clear thesis?
- ✔ Does each sentence contain specificity?
- ✔ Do my paragraphs have continuity by using appropriate transitions?
- ✔ Did I avoid redundancy?
- ✔ Did I cite the document correctly? The Fugitive Slave Law threatened the freedom of African Americans living in the north. (Fugitive Slave Law, September 18, 1850)
- ✔ Is the information consistent with my thesis?
- ✔ Does the last sentence of each paragraph pave the way for the next paragraph?
- ✔ Does the conclusion restate the thesis?

Whether you have the time to carefully revise your work or need to revise on the run, **reading between the lines** of your own writing is a critical step in writing clear and powerful document-based essays.

# The DBQ Self-Evaluation

**H**ave you ever finished a baseball game and thought you could have played better? Have you ever gotten a test back and wondered why you did so well? As we go through our daily activities, we are constantly evaluating ourselves. Though we may not realize it, we are very critical of ourselves. We recognize when we are not successful, and feel a sense of accomplishment when we are. Evaluation is an appropriate tool to use to measure where we are and where we want to be. By evaluating ourselves, we can recognize our strengths and weaknesses and set realistic goals.

To evaluate your DBQ, you'll want to ask yourself questions like those listed below. Your answers will enable you to evaluate how successful you are at writing the DBQ. This in turn, will allow you to set realistic goals for achieving a higher score on the assessment rubric.

*Questions on a DBQ Self-Evaluation checklist include questions like these:*
 - ✔ What part(s) of the DBQ were you able to complete successfully? Why?
 - ✔ What part(s) of the DBQ did you find difficult? Why?
 - ✔ What will your score be on the 1–5 rubric for the DBQ?
 - ✔ What steps can you take to improve your score on the rubric?
 - ✔ What part of the DBQ do you find to be the most difficult? Why?

*How do you know you have completed the DBQ Self-Evaluation correctly?*

1. **What part(s) of the DBQ were you able to complete successfully? Why?**

   When answering this question, you should begin to review each part of the DBQ. Which part (introduction, thesis statement, body paragraphs, document information, outside information, conclusion) of the DBQ did you feel confident writing? What enabled you to have this confidence? Try to focus on the factors that caused you to be successful. By focusing on these factors, you will be able to perfect them, therefore, achieving a higher score on the DBQ rubric.

2. **What part(s) of the DBQ did you find difficult? Why?**

   Identify the part(s) of the DBQ you had difficulty with. What caused you this difficulty? Go back through the chapters where the particular section you are having difficulty with is discussed. Read through the information on that section carefully. Look at the samples that were provided for that section. Try to model the samples. Remember, you do not have to work alone. If you are still having difficulty with the section, ask an adult or a friend who feels confident with this particular section.

3. **What will your score be on the 1–5 rubric for the DBQ?**

   Use the assessment rubric in Chapter 10 to determine your score. If your score falls below a 3, you should consider using the revision strategies discussed in Chapter 7 to help you achieve a higher rubric score. If your score is a 3 or above, you may also use the revision strategies to enable you to achieve a higher score on the assessment rubric. There is always room for improvement. By using all of the writing suggestions given in this book along with your hard work and determination, you will become a successful writer.

4. **What steps can you take to improve your score on the rubric?**

   When trying to improve your score on the assessment rubric, you should begin by reading your writing aloud. Put yourself in the position of the reader or audience. Have you included all the important information about your subject? Do you understand what you have written? Are your ideas clear and complete? Are your ideas organized? Have you included document information? Have you included outside information? Is there enough detail? Is the writing interesting? If someone else had given you this piece of writing to read, would you enjoy reading it? Why or Why not?

   Try differentiating the strong parts of your essay from the weak parts. First, identify the strong parts of the essay. Underline the parts that you like. What makes those parts strong? Then, identify the weak parts of your essay. Highlight the weak parts. Go back to the part of the chapters that explain this specific problem in depth. For example, if you are having trouble writing an effective thesis statement, go back and read the section in Chapter 6 that explains how to write a thesis statement. Use the examples given in this section to help you write a thesis statement. Using the revision strategies discussed in Chapter 7 will also help you write a more effective essay. After you have used the examples and the revision strategies to improve your writing, read your writing aloud once again. Are you completely satisfied with your essay? If not, you may repeat the revision again. If so, you may begin writing your final copy.

5. **What part of the DBQ do you find to be the most difficult? Why?**

   Try to identify the part of the DBQ you are having the most difficulty with. Chances are, this is the problem that is most likely to result in a low rubric score and this is the section that will require the most revision. Be persistent. Once again, use the revision strategies. Go back and read the section for that particular part. Try to model the examples given. The more time and effort you put into your writing skills, the more successful you will be.

By using self-evaluation to evaluate your document-based essay, you will identify your strengths and weaknesses. Knowing your strengths and weaknesses will help you to successfully use the revision strategies to achieve a higher score on the assessment rubric.

# Sample Document-Based Essays

**T**his chapter will provide you with five document-based essays. These DBQs were designed for you to practice your test-taking skills. They represent how a DBQ might appear on an assessment exam. When answering these DBQs, use all of the skills you were taught in the previous chapters. If you need to review, go back and reread the chapters that will enable you to successfully respond to these DBQs. When you finish, check the Answer Key on page 202.

## ▶ DOCUMENT-BASED QUESTION: THE U.S. CONSTITUTION

The following document-based question is based on the accompanying documents numbered 1–7. The DBQ is designed to test your ability to work with historical documents. As you analyze the documents, take into account both the context of each document and any point of view that may be presented in the document.

**Theme:** The U.S. Constitution

**Historical Context:** After the American Revolution, the Articles of Confederation governed the new nation. This new government created a loose alliance of the newly independent states. Many Americans were suspicious of a central government, fearing that power concentrated in a central government could threaten their freedom. The creation of a weak central government almost led to the failure of the new nation. Under the Articles of Confederation, Congress could not regulate trade between the states or with foreign nations, nor did they have the power to tax. As inflation began to rise and the country entered a period of economic distress, the leaders of the new nation realized the need for a new form of government, one which would be stronger than the Articles of Confederation, yet balance authority in an attempt to protect the rights of American citizens. During the Constitutional Convention of 1787, the U.S. Constitution was born. This powerful document was designed to equally delegate power between the federal and state governments, while at the same time, protect American citizens from tyranny. This new government would never be able to abuse its power and infringe upon the rights of its citizens the way Great Britain infringed upon the rights of the colonists.

**Task:** Write an essay explaining how the U.S. Constitution protects or safeguards the rights of American citizens.

## PART A: SCAFFOLDING QUESTIONS

Analyze each of the following documents and answer the scaffolding questions that follow each document in the space provided.

## DOCUMENT 1

## *The First Amendment*

Congress shall make no law respecting an establishment of religion, or prohibiting the free exercise thereof; or **abridging** (limiting) the freedom of speech, or of the press; or the right of the people peaceably to assemble, and to **petition** (ask) the government for a **redress** (correction) of **grievances** (wrongs).

*Source:* The Bill of Rights

**1.** The First Amendment entitles Americans to what rights?

_____

_____

_____

**2.** According to the First Amendment, why would Americans petition the government?

_____

_____

_____

_____

_____

## DOCUMENT 2

### The Fourth Amendment

The right of the people to be **secure** (safe) in their persons, houses, papers, and effects, against unreasonable searches and seizures, shall not be **violated**; and no **warrants** (an order from a judge authorizing an arrest or a search and seizure) shall issue but upon **probable** (likely) cause, supported by **oath** (promise) or **affirmation** (confirmation), and particularly describing the place to be searched, and the persons or things to be seized.

_Source:_ The Bill of Rights

**1.** The Fourth Amendment entitles Americans to what rights?

_____

_____

_____

_____

**2.** Under what terms can a judge issue a warrant?

_____

_____

_____

_____

## DOCUMENT 3

## *The Fifth Amendment*

No person shall be held to answer for a **capital** (capital crimes are punishable by death), or otherwise **infamous crime** (crimes which carry a prison sentence or cause you to lose some of your rights), unless on a presentment or **indictment** (formal accusation) of a grand jury, except in cases arising in the land or naval forces, or in the militia, when in actual service in time of war or public danger; nor shall any person be subject for the same offense to be twice put in **jeopardy** (danger) of life and limb; nor shall be **compelled** (forced), in any criminal case, to be a witness against himself; nor be **deprived** of life, liberty, or property, without due process of law; nor shall private property be taken for public use, without just **compensation** (payment).

*Source:* The Bill of Rights

**1.** The Fifth Amendment entitles Americans to what rights?

_____

_____

_____

_____

_____

**2.** When can a person be held answerable for a capital crime?

_____

_____

_____

_____

_____

## DOCUMENT 4

### *The Fifteenth Amendment*

The right of citizens of the United States to vote shall not be denied or **abridged** (limited) by the United States or any state on the account of race, color, or previous condition of **servitude** (slavery).

*Source:* The Bill of Rights

**1.** What was the purpose of the Fifteenth Amendment?

_____

_____

_____

_____

**2.** How did this amendment change the lives of African-American men?

_____

_____

_____

_____

# DOCUMENT 5

## *The U.S. Constitution, Article 5*

The Congress, whenever two-thirds of both houses shall deem it necessary, shall propose **amendments** (changes) to this Constitution, or, on the application of the **legislatures** (law-making bodies; the legislature of the United States government consists of the House of Representatives and the Senate) of two-thirds of the several states, shall call a **convention** (meeting) for proposing amendments, which, in either case, shall be **valid** to all intents and purposes, as part of this Constitution, when **ratified** (approved) by the legislatures of three-fourths of the several states, or by conventions in three-fourths thereof, as the one or the other mode of ratification may be proposed by the Congress; provided that no amendments which may be made prior to the year 1808 shall in any manner affect the first and fourth clauses in the Ninth Section of the First Article; and that no state, without its consent shall be **deprived** of its equal **suffrage** (vote) in the Senate.

*Source:* HistoryCentral.com

**1.** Where can an amendment to the Constitution be introduced?

_____

_____

_____

_____

**2.** How is an amendment to the U.S. Constitution ratified?

_____

_____

_____

_____

## DOCUMENT 6

## *The Tenth Amendment*

The powers not **delegated** (given to) to the United States by the Constitution, nor **prohibited** (forbidden) by it to the states, are **reserved** (set aside) to the states respectively, or to the people.

*Source:* The Bill of Rights

**1.** What are delegated powers?

_____

_____

_____

_____

**2.** What powers are given to the states?

_____

_____

_____

_____

## DOCUMENT 7

## *The Nineteenth Amendment*

The right of citizens of the United States to vote shall not be denied or **abridged** (limited) by the United States or by any state on the account of sex.

*Source:* The Bill of Rights

**1.** What is the purpose of the Nineteenth Amendment?

_____

_____

_____

_____

**2.** What group(s) was/were given the right to vote under the Nineteenth Amendment?

_____

_____

_____

_____

## PART B: THE ESSAY

**Directions:** Write a well-organized essay that includes the following:

A. **Introduction:** Your introduction must address the theme of the document-based question and should include a hook. The historical context, as well as necessary background information, may be used as part of your introduction. Your thesis statement must be included in your introduction.

B. **Body:** For each body paragraph, explain how the U.S. Constitution protects or safeguards the rights of American citizens. Each body paragraph should contain at least one of the documents, as well as outside information, to support your answer to the task question.

C. **Conclusion:** In the conclusion, restate your thesis and summarize the main ideas of your essay. Try to leave the reader with a lasting impression of the topic or theme.

**Historical Context:** After the American Revolution, the Articles of Confederation governed the new nation. This new government created a loose alliance of the newly independent states. Many Americans were suspicious of a central government, fearing that power concentrated in a central government could threaten their freedom. The creation of a weak central government almost lead to the failure of the new nation. Under the Articles of Confederation, Congress could not regulate trade between the states or with foreign nations, nor did they have the power to tax. As inflation began to rise and the country entered a period of economic distress, the leaders of the new nation realized the need for a new form a government, one which would be stronger than the Articles of Confederation, yet balance authority in an attempt to protect the rights of American citizens. During the Constitutional Convention of 1787, the U.S. Constitution was born. This powerful document was designed to equally delegate power between the federal and state governments, while at the same time, protect American citizens from tyranny. This new government would never be able to abuse its power and infringe upon the rights of its citizens the way Great Britain infringed upon the rights of the colonists.

**Task:** Write an essay explaining how the U.S. Constitution protects the rights of American citizens.

Be sure to include specific details! You must also use additional information from your knowledge of social studies.

_____

_____

_____

_____

_____

# ▶ DOCUMENT-BASED QUESTION: THE AMERICAN REVOLUTION

This document-based question is based on the accompanying documents numbered 1–5. The DBQ is designed to test your ability to work with historical documents. As you analyze the documents, take into account both the context of each document and any point of view that may be presented in the document.

**Theme:** The American Revolution
**Task:** Write an essay in which you explain why the colonists were justified in breaking away from Great Britain.

**Historical Context:** During the years 1763–1776, there was a series of events that created conflict between the American colonies and Great Britain. Since the beginning of their existence, the colonies always had a voice in government and were able to contribute to their economic success without any interference from Great Britain. The American colonists believed Great Britain was creating and enforcing laws, which violated the rights of the colonists. The colonists took the position that not having a voice in the British Parliament was unjust. Great Britain believed her colonies should be loyal subjects since it was Great Britain who was supporting and protecting the colonies. The differing points of view between Great Britain and the American colonies led to a series of conflicts between the two. The ultimate result of this conflict was the termination of the relationship between the colonies and the mother country and the emergence of a new nation, the United States of America.

## PART A: SCAFFOLDING QUESTIONS

Analyze each of the following documents and answer the scaffolding questions that follow each document in the space provided.

## DOCUMENT 1

### *The Royal Proclamation of 1763*

And we do further **declare** (state) it be our royal will and pleasure, for the present, as **aforesaid** (mentioned before), to reserve under our **sovereignty** (power), protection and **dominion** (control), for the use of the said Indian lands, all the land and territories not included within the limits of our said three new government (Quebec, East Florida, and West Florida), or within the limits granted to the Hudson Bay Company; as also all of the land and territories lying to the westward of the sources of the rivers which fall into the sea from the west and the northwest as aforesaid.

Persons who have **inadvertently** (accidentally) settled upon such reserved lands to remove. No sale of Indian lands to be allowed, except to the Crown. The Indian trade to be free to English subjects, under license from the governor or commander in chief of some colony. Fugitives from justice, taking refuge (place of safety) in this reserved territory, to be **apprehended** (caught) and returned.

*Source:* HistoryCentral.com

**1.** According to the Royal Proclamation of 1763, what would happen to those who were considered fugitives?

_____

_____

_____

_____

_____

**2.** How did the Royal Proclamation of 1763 restrict the rights of the Colonists?

_____

_____

_____

_____

_____

## DOCUMENT 2

### *The Declaratory Act*

That the said colonies and plantations in America have been, are, and of right ought to be, **subordinate** (inferior) unto, and dependent upon the imperial crown and parliament of Great Britain; and that the King's Majesty, by and with the advice and **consent** (agreement) of the lords spiritual and **temporal** (worldly), and commons of Great Britain, in parliament assembled, had, hath, and of right ought to have, full power and authority to make laws and statutes of sufficient force and validity, to bind the colonies and people of America, subjects of the crown of Great Britain, in all cases whatsoever.

*Source:* HistoryCentral.com

**1.** How did the Declaratory Act increase Great Britain's power over the colonists?

_____

_____

_____

_____

**2.** How could this act lead to a violation of rights?

_____

_____

_____

_____

# DOCUMENT 3

## *Paul Revere's Engraving*

*Source:* HistoryCentral.com

**1.** Which two groups are presented in the engraving?

_____

_____

_____

_____

**2.** Which group is demonstrating an abuse of power? Why?

_____

_____

_____

_____

## *Colonial Legislation*

| Act | Date | Effect on Colonists |
|---|---|---|
| Stamp Act | 1765 | All legal documents, newspapers, almanacs, playing cards, and dice were taxed. |
| Townshend Acts | 1767 | A tax was placed on lead, glass, paper, paint, and tea. British officers used writs of assistance to search and seize a ship's cargo if there was suspicion of smuggled goods. |
| Tea Act | 1773 | British East India company sold tea directly to the colonists. Colonial tea merchants were eliminated from the tea trade. |

**1.** How did these acts affect colonial life?

_____

_____

_____

_____

**2.** How did the British attempt to control the amount of goods smuggled into the colonies?

_____

_____

_____

_____

## DOCUMENT 5

### *The Intolerable Acts*

1. The port of Boston was closed to all trade until the colonists paid for the tea destroyed during the Boston Tea Party.
2. Colonists in Massachusetts could not hold town meetings more than once a year without the governor's permission.
3. British customs officials, as well as other British officials, charged with committing major crimes in the colonies would be tried in Great Britain, not Massachusetts.
4. A quartering act was passed forcing Massachusetts colonists to house British soldiers in their home.

**1.** How did the Intolerable Acts punish the Massachusetts colonists for the Boston Tea Party?

_____

_____

_____

_____

**2.** How did these acts impact the economy of Massachusetts?

_____

_____

_____

_____

## DOCUMENT 6

We hold these truths to be **self-evident** (easy to see), that all men are created equal; that they are endowed by their **Creator** (God) with certain **unalienable rights** (rights that cannot be taken away); that among these are life, liberty, and the pursuit of happiness. That to secure these rights, governments are **instituted** (established) among men, **deriving** (receiving) their just powers from the **consent** (permission) of the governed; that, whenever any form of government becomes destructive of these ends, it is the right of the people to alter or **abolish** (end) it, and to institute a new government, laying its foundation on such principles and organizing its powers in such form, as to them shall seem most likely to effect their safety and happiness.

*Source:* HistoryCentral.com

**1.** Where does government get the right to rule?

_____

_____

_____

_____

**2.** If the government does not listen to its people, what do the people have a right to do?

_____

_____

_____

_____

_____

## PART B: THE ESSAY

**Directions:** Write a well-organized essay that includes the following:

A. **Introduction:** Your introduction must address the theme of the document-based question and should include a hook. The historical context, as well as necessary background information, may be used as part of your introduction. Your thesis statement must be included in your introduction.

B. **Body:** For each body paragraph, explain why the colonists were justified in breaking away from Great Britain. Each body paragraph should contain at least one of the documents, as well as outside information, to support your answer to the task question.

C. **Conclusion:** In the conclusion, restate your thesis and summarize the main ideas of your essay. Try to leave the reader with a lasting impression of the topic or theme.

**Historical Context:** During the years 1763–1776, there were a series of events that created conflict between the American colonies and Great Britain. Since the beginning of their existence, the colonies always had a voice in government and were able to contribute to their economic success without any interference from Great Britain. The American colonists believed Great Britain was creating and enforcing laws, which violated the rights of the colonists. The colonists took the position that not having a voice in the British Parliament was unjust. Great Britain believed her colonies should be loyal subjects since it was Great Britain who was supporting and protecting the colonies. The differing points of view between Great Britain and the American colonies led to a series of conflicts between the two. The ultimate result of this conflict was the termination of the relationship between the colonies and the mother country and the emergence of a new nation—the United States of America.

**Task:** Write an essay in which you explain why the colonists were justified in breaking away from Great Britain.

Be sure to include specific details. You must also use additional information from your knowledge of social studies.

_____

_____

_____

_____

_____

_____

_____

# ▶ DOCUMENT-BASED QUESTION: THE PROGRESSIVE ERA

This document-based question is based on the accompanying documents numbered 1–7. The DBQ is designed to test your ability to work with historical documents. As you analyze the documents, take into account both the context of each document and any point of view that may be presented in the document.

**Theme:** The Progressive Era

**Historical Context:** The Progressive Era emerged in the late 1800s. The Progressives felt a need for change in American society and worked toward achieving various social, political, and economic reforms. They fought against corruption in government and worked to reduce the power of monopolies. During the Progressive Era, there was a heightened awareness of issues such as women's suffrage and child labor. Muckrakers used journalism as a means to change public opinion on the need for reform. Though African Americans never truly achieved equal status until the Civil Rights Movement, it was during the Progressive Era that action was first taken against racial discrimination.

**Task:** Write an essay in which you explain four ways in which the Progressives attempted to reform American society.

## PART A: SCAFFOLDING QUESTIONS

Analyze each of the following documents and answer the scaffolding questions that follow each document in the space provided.

### DOCUMENT 1

**Child Laborers in Indiana Glass Works, Midnight, Indiana. 1908.**

*Source:* The National Archives and Records Administration

**1.** What are the children in the picture doing?

_____

_____

_____

_____

_____

**2.** What dangers were these children exposed to while working in this factory?

_____

_____

_____

_____

_____

## DOCUMENT 2

## *The Fifteenth Amendment*

The right of citizens of the United States to vote shall not be denied or **abridged** (limited) by the United States or any state on the account of race, color, or previous condition of **servitude** (slavery).

*Source:* The Bill of Rights

**1.** What was the purpose of the Fifteenth Amendment?

_____

_____

_____

_____

**2.** How did this amendment change the lives of African Americans?

_____

_____

_____

_____

_____

## The Eighteenth Amendment: Prohibition of Alcoholic Beverages

After one year from the **ratification** (approval) of this article the manufacture, sale, or transportation of intoxicating liquors within, the importation thereof into, or the exportation thereof from, the United States and all territory subject to the **jurisdiction** (authority) thereof for beverage purposes is hereby prohibited.

*Source:* Bill of Rights

**1.** What did the Eighteenth Amendment prohibit?

_____

_____

_____

_____

**2.** What impact did this amendment have on American society?

_____

_____

_____

_____

## DOCUMENT 4

*Sources:* The Library of Congress and www.library.ucla.edu/libraries/college/research/reference/images.htm

**1.** What are the women in the photograph asking for?

**2.** Who are the women targeting in an effort to win suffrage?

## DOCUMENT 5

## Legislative Acts of the Progressive Era

| Act | Date | Explanation |
|-----|------|-------------|
| Meat Inspection Act | 1906 | Ensured clean conditions regarding meat processing; federal inspection of such facilities is required. |
| Pendleton Act | 1883 | Exams for federal jobs are now conducted by a civil service commission to fill jobs on the basis of merit. |
| Pure Food and Drug Act | 1906 | Labeling of food and drugs had to be truthful and accurate. |
| Sherman Anti-trust Act | 1890 | Monopolies and trusts were outlawed. |

**1.** Which acts provided health regulations for the safety of food production?

_____

_____

_____

_____

**2.** How did these legislative acts improve American society?

_____

_____

_____

_____

## *The Nineteenth Amendment*

The right of citizens of the United States to vote shall not be denied or **abridged** (limited) by the United States or by any state on the account of sex.

*Source:* The Bill of Rights

**1.** What was the purpose of the Nineteenth Amendment?

_____

_____

_____

_____

**2.** How did the Nineteenth Amendment change the role of women in American society?

_____

_____

_____

_____

## DOCUMENT 7

## *The Seventeenth Amendment*

The Senate of the United States shall be composed of two Senators from each state, elected by the people thereof, for six years; and each Senator shall have one vote. The electors in each state shall have the qualifications **requisite** (requirement) for electors of the most numerous branch of the state legislatures.

*Source:* The Bill of Rights

**1.** How are United States Senators elected?

_____

_____

_____

_____

_____

**2.** How did this amendment give more power to the American people?

_____

_____

_____

_____

_____

## PART B: THE ESSAY

**Directions:** Write a well-organized essay that includes the following:

A. **Introduction:** Your introduction must address the theme of the document-based question and should include a hook. The historical context, as well as necessary background information, may be used as part of your introduction. Your thesis statement must be included in your introduction.

B. **Body:** For each body paragraph, explain one way in which the Progressives attempted to reform American society. Each body paragraph should contain at least one of the documents, as well as outside information, to support your answer to the task question.

C. **Conclusion:** In the conclusion, restate your thesis and summarize the main ideas of your essay. Try to leave the reader with a lasting impression of the topic or theme.

**Historical Context:** The Progressive Era emerged in the late 1800s. The Progressives felt a need for change in American society and worked toward achieving various social, political, and economic reforms. They fought against corruption in government and worked to reduce the power of monopolies. During the Progressive Era, there was a heightened awareness of issues such as women's suffrage and child labor. Muckrakers used journalism as a means to change public opinion on the need for reform. Though African Americans never truly achieved equal status until the Civil Rights Movement, it was during the Progressive Era that action was first taken against racial discrimination.

**Task:** Write an essay in which you explain four ways in which the Progressives attempted to reform American society.

Be sure to include specific details. You must also use additional information from your knowledge of social studies.

_____

_____

_____

_____

_____

_____

_____

_____

# ▶ DOCUMENT-BASED QUESTION: THE CIVIL WAR

This document-based question is based on the accompanying documents numbered 1–5. The DBQ is designed to test your ability to work with historical documents. As you analyze the documents, take into account both the context of each document and any point of view that may be presented in the document.

**Theme:** The Civil War

**Historical Context:** Since the beginning of the colonial era, slaves were used to fill the need for an inexpensive source of labor in America. In the period of 1861–1865, the United States was engulfed in a civil war. Standing at the heart of the Civil War was the issue of slavery. The South, whose economy was greatly dependent on the institution of slavery, wanted to leave the Union and become an independent nation. The North, whose greatest advantage was industrial resources, believed they had to fight to preserve the Union. Though initially Northerners did not believe the goal of the war to be the issue of freeing slaves, the Emancipation Proclamation changed the purpose of the war. Northerners now not only fought to preserve the Union, they fought to abolish one of the greatest violations of human rights: the institution of slavery.

**Task:** Write an essay in which you explain whether or not slavery was an acceptable form of labor in the South.

## PART A: SCAFFOLDING QUESTIONS

Analyze each of the following documents and answer the scaffolding questions that follow each document in the space provided.

## DOCUMENT 1

## *The Confederate Constitution, Section 9*

No **bill of attainder** (a legal act taking away a person's property if they are found guilty of a felony or treason), **ex post facto law** (a law imposing a punishment for an act that was legal at the time it was committed), or law denying or impairing the right of property in Negro slaves shall be passed.

*Source:* HistoryCentral.com

**1.** According to the Confederate Constitution, what position did a slave hold in American society?

_____

_____

_____

_____

_____

**2.** How did Section 9 of the Confederate Constitution protect the institution of slavery?

_____

_____

_____

_____

_____

It may, in truth, be assumed as **maxim** (truth), that two races differing so greatly, and in so many respects, cannot possibly exist together in the same country, where their numbers are nearly equal, without one being **subjected** (under the control of) to the other. Experience has proved that the existing relation, in which the one is subjected to the other, in the slaveholding States, is consistent with the peace and safety of both, with great improvement to the **inferior** (not equal to); while the same experience proves that . . . the **abolition** (end) of slavery would (if it did not destroy the inferior by conflicts, to which it would lead) reduce it to the extremes of **vice** (evil behavior) and **wretchedness** (meanness). In this view of the subject, it may be asserted, that what is called slavery is in reality a political institution, essential to the peace, safety, and **prosperity** (success) of those States of the Union in which it exists.

—John C. Calhoun

*Source:* HistoryCentral.com

**1.** What is John C. Calhoun's position on slavery?

_____

_____

_____

_____

**2.** What does he believe will happen if slavery is abolished?

_____

_____

_____

_____

## DOCUMENT 3

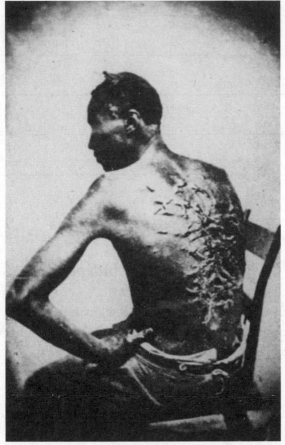

"Overseer Artayou Carrier whipped me. I was two months in bed sore from the whip-ping. My master come after I was whipped; he discharged the overseer. The very words of poor Peter, taken as he sat for his picture." Baton Rouge, LA, April 2, 1863.

*Source:* National Archives and Records Administration

**1.** According to the photograph, how were slaves treated by their overseers?

_____

_____

_____

_____

_____

**2.** How did the master of this slave react to this kind of treatment?

_____

_____

_____

_____

_____

## DOCUMENT 4

### *The Declaration of Independence*

We hold these truths to be **self-evident** (easy to see), that all men are created equal; that they are **endowed** (given) by their **Creator** (God) with certain unalienable rights (natural rights which cannot be taken away); that among these are life, liberty, and the pursuit of happiness.

*Source:* HistoryCentral.com

**1.** According to the Declaration of Independence, how are all men created?

_____

_____

_____

_____

**2.** What rights are all men entitled to?

_____

_____

_____

_____

## DOCUMENT 5

### *The Emancipation Proclamation*

"And by virtue of the power and for the purpose **aforesaid** (mentioned before), I do order and **declare** (state) that all persons held as slaves within said **designated** (chosen) states (states fighting against the Union) and parts of states are, and **henceforward** (after this) shall be, free; and that the Executive Government of the United States, including the military and naval authorities thereof, will recognize and maintain the freedom of said persons.

And I hereby enjoin upon the people so declared to be free and **abstain** (withhold) from all violence, unless in necessary self-defense; and I recommend to them that, in all cases when allowed, they labor faithfully for reasonable wages.

And I further declare and make known that such persons, of suitable condition, will be received into the armed service of the United States to garrison forts, positions, stations, and other places, and to man vessels of all sorts in said service."

*Source:* HistoryCentral.com

**1.** How did the Emancipation Proclamation change the institution of slavery in America?

_____

_____

_____

_____

**2.** According to the Emancipation Proclamation, what was expected of the newly freed slaves?

_____

_____

_____

_____

## PART B: THE ESSAY

**Directions:** Write a well-organized essay that includes the following:

A.  **Introduction:** Your introduction must address the theme of the document-based question and should include a hook. The historical context, as well as necessary background information, may be used as part of your introduction. Your thesis statement must be included in your introduction.

B.  **Body:** For each body paragraph, explain whether or not slavery was an acceptable form of labor in the South. Each body paragraph should contain at least one of the documents as evidence, as well as outside information, to support your answer to the task question.

C.  **Conclusion:** In the conclusion, restate your thesis and summarize the main ideas of your essay. Try to leave the reader with a lasting impression of the topic or theme.

**Historical Context:** Since the beginning of the colonial era, slaves were used to fill the need for an inexpensive source of labor in America. In the period of 1861–1865, the United States was engulfed in a civil war. Standing at the heart of the Civil War was the issue of slavery. The South, whose economy was greatly dependent on the institution of slavery, wanted to leave the Union and become an independent nation. The North, whose industrial resources were their greatest advantage, believed they had to fight to preserve the Union. Though initially Northerners did not believe the goal of the war to be the issue of freeing slaves, the Emancipation Proclamation changed the purpose of the war. Northerners now not only fought to preserve the Union, they fought to abolish one of the greatest violations of human rights; the institution of slavery.

**Task:** Write an essay in which you explain whether or not slavery was an acceptable form of labor in the South.

Be sure to include specific details. You must also use additional information from your knowledge of social studies.

_____

_____

_____

_____

_____

_____

_____

_____

# ▶ DOCUMENT-BASED QUESTION: WORLD WAR II

This document-based question is based on the accompanying documents numbered 1–5. The DBQ is designed to test your ability to work with historical documents. As you analyze the documents, take into account both the context of each document and any point of view that may be presented in the document.

**Theme:** World War II

**Historical Context:** After the bombing of Pearl Harbor on December 7, 1941, the United States entered one of its darkest periods in history. The involvement of the United States in World War II would forever change American society. The attack on Pearl Harbor led many Americans to turn against their fellow Japanese-Americans. The reality of war contributed to the already-existing harsh economic conditions. As men traded their daily occupations for the battlefield, women became a dominant force in the working world. Every American citizen was called upon to contribute to the war effort. A strong sense of nationalism was sweeping across a bewildered nation.

**Task:** Write an essay to explain three ways in which World War II changed American society.

_____

_____

_____

_____

_____

_____

_____

_____

_____

_____

## PART A: SCAFFOLDING QUESTIONS

Analyze each of the following documents and answer the scaffolding questions that follow each document in the space provided.

## DOCUMENT 1

### *President Frankliin D. Roosevelt*

We are now in this war. We are all in it—all the way. Every single man, woman, and child is a partner in the most tremendous undertaking of our American history. We must share together the bad news and the good news, the defeats and the victories—the changing fortunes of war.

*Source:* HistoryCentral.com

1. According to President Roosevelt, who is involved in the war?

_____

_____

_____

_____

2. How will this war affect every American?

_____

_____

_____

_____

*Source:* National Archives and Records Administration

**1.** Which group of Americans is this poster addressing?

_____

_____

_____

_____

_____

**2.** According to the poster, how did the role of women change during World War II?

_____

_____

_____

_____

## Radio Address of President Franklin D. Roosevelt, October 12, 1942

This whole nation of one hundred and thirty million free men, women, and children is becoming one great fighting force. Some of us are soldiers or sailors, some of us are civilians. Some of us are fighting the war in airplanes five miles above the continent of Europe or on the islands of the Pacific—and some of us are fighting in mines deep down in the earth of Pennsylvania or Montana. A few of us are decorated with medals for heroic achievement, but all of us can have that deep and permanent inner satisfaction that comes from doing the best we know how—each of us playing an honorable part in the great struggle to save our democratic civilization.

*Source:* HistoryCentral.com

**1.** According to the radio address, how were Americans helping the war effort?

_____

_____

_____

_____

_____

**2.** How would this effort preserve American democracy?

_____

_____

_____

_____

_____

# DOCUMENT 4

## *A Japanese Grocery Store*

"Following evacuation orders, this store was closed. The owner, a University of California graduate of Japanese descent, placed the I AM AN AMERICAN sign on the storefront after Pearl Harbor." Oakland, CA, April 1942. Dorothea Lange.

*Source:* National Archives and Records Administration

1. Why was this Japanese grocery store closed?

_____

_____

_____

_____

**2.** Why was the sign, "I AM AN AMERICAN" placed on the storefront?

_____

_____

_____

_____

_____

## DOCUMENT 5

*Source:* National Archives and Records Administration

**1.** What item in this photograph is being rationed?

_____

_____

_____

_____

**2.** Why would this product be rationed during World War II?

_____

_____

_____

_____

## PART B: THE ESSAY

**Directions:** Write a well-organized essay that includes the following:

A. **Introduction:** Your introduction must address the theme of the document-based question and should include a hook. The historical context, as well as necessary background information, may be used as part of your introduction. Your thesis statement must be included in your introduction.

B. **Body:** For each body paragraph, explain one way in which World War II changed American society. Each body paragraph should contain at least one of the documents, as well as outside information, to support your answer to the task question.

C. **Conclusion:** In the conclusion, restate your thesis and summarize the main ideas of your essay. Try to leave the reader with a lasting impression of the topic or theme.

**Historical Context:** After the bombing of Pearl Harbor on December 7, 1941, the United States entered one of its darkest periods in history. The involvement of the United States in World War II would forever change American society. The attack on Pearl Harbor led many Americans to turn against their fellow Japanese-Americans. The reality of war contributed to the already existing harsh economic conditions. As men traded their daily occupations for those of a soldier, women became a dominant force in the working world. Every American citizen was called upon to contribute to the war effort. A strong sense of nationalism was sweeping across a bewildered nation.

**Task:** Write an essay to explain three ways in which World War II changed American society.

Be sure to include specific details. You must also use additional information from your knowledge of social studies.

_____

_____

_____

_____

_____

_____

_____

## DOCUMENT-BASED QUESTION:
## THE UNITED STATES CONSTITUTION

| Document 1<br>The First Amendment | Scaffolding Questions<br>and Answers |
|---|---|
| Congress shall make no law respecting an establishment of religion, or prohibiting the free exercise thereof; or **abridging** (limiting) the freedom of speech, or of the press; or the right of the people peaceably to assemble, and to **petition** (ask) the government for a **redress** (correction) of **grievances** (wrongs).<br><br>*Source:* The Bill of Rights | 1. **The First Amendment entitles us to what rights?** The First Amendment entitles Americans to such rights as freedom of religion, freedom of speech, freedom of the press, freedom of assembly, and the right to petition the government to correct any wrongs.<br>2. **According to the First Amendment, why would Americans petition the government?** According to the First Amendment, Americans would petition the government to ask for a correction of any wrongs. |

| Document 2<br>The Fourth Amendment | Scaffolding Questions<br>and Answers |
|---|---|
| The right of the people to be **secure** (safe) in their persons, houses, papers, and effects, against unreasonable searches and seizures, shall not be **violated**; and no **warrants** (an order from a judge authorizing an arrest or a search and seizure) shall issue but upon **probable** (likely) cause, supported by **oath** (promise) or **affirmation** (confirmation), and particularly describing the place to be searched, and the persons or things to be seized.<br><br>*Source:* The Bill of Rights | 1. **The Fourth Amendment entitles Americans to what rights?** The Fourth Amendment entitles Americans to protection against illegal search and seizure.<br>2. **Under what terms can a judge issue a warrant?** A judge can only issue a warrant if there is probable cause. |

| Document 3<br>The Fifth Amendment | Scaffolding Questions<br>and Answers |
|---|---|
| No person shall be held to answer for a **capital** (capital crimes are punishable by death), or otherwise **infamous crime** (crimes which carry a prison sentence or cause you to lose some of your rights), unless on a presentment or **indictment** (formal accusation) of a grand jury, except in cases arising in the land or naval forces, or in the militia, when in actual service in time of war or public danger; nor shall any person be subject for the same offense to be twice put in **jeopardy** (danger) of life and limb; nor shall be **compelled** (forced), in any criminal case, to be a witness against himself; nor be **deprived** of life, liberty, or property, without due process of law; nor shall private property be taken for public use, without just **compensation** (payment).<br>*Source:* The Bill of Rights | 1. **The Fifth Amendment entitles Americans to what rights?** Americans must be indicted by a grand jury before they can be prosecuted for a crime. Americans cannot be tried twice for the same crime. Americans do not have to testify against themselves. If any property is seized, the government must pay the owner a fair price for it.<br>2. **When can a person be held answerable for a capital crime?** A person is responsible for answering to a capital crime when an indictment from a grand jury is obtained. |

| Document 4<br>The Fifteenth Amendment | Scaffolding Questions<br>and Answers |
|---|---|
| The right of citizens of the United States to vote shall not be denied or **abridged** (limited) by the United States or any state on the account of race, color, or previous condition of **servitude** (slavery).<br>*Source:* The Bill of Rights | 1. **What was the purpose of the Fifteenth Amendment?** The purpose of the Fifteenth Amendment was to give African Americans the right to vote.<br>2. **How did this amendment change the lives of African-American men?** This amendment changed the lives of African-American men by giving them the legal right to have a say in government. |

| Document 5<br>The United States Constitution, Article 5 | Scaffolding Questions<br>and Answers |
|---|---|
| The Congress, whenever two-thirds of both houses shall deem it necessary, shall propose **amendments** (changes) to this Constitution, or, on the application of the **legislatures** (law-making bodies. The legislature of the United States government consists of the House of Representatives and the Senate) of two-thirds of the several states, shall call a **convention** (meeting) for proposing amendments, which, in either case, shall be **valid** to all intents and purposes, as part of this Constitution, when **ratified** (approved) by the legislatures of three-fourths of the several states, or by conventions in three-fourths thereof, as the one or the other mode of ratification may be proposed by the Congress; provided that no amendments which may be made prior to the year 1808 shall in any manner affect the first and fourth clauses in the Ninth Section of the First Article; and that no state, without its consent shall be **deprived** of its equal **suffrage** (vote) in the Senate.<br>*Source:* HistoryCentral.com | 1. **Where can an amendment to the Constitution be introduced?** An amendment to the Constitution can be introduced by a two-thirds vote of both houses of Congress or by a national convention called by Congress at the request of two-thirds of the state legislatures.<br>2. **How is an amendment to the United States Constitution ratified?** An amendment is ratified when three-fourths of the state legislatures or special conventions in three-fourths of the states agree to it. |

| Document 6<br>The Tenth Amendment | Scaffolding Questions<br>and Answers |
|---|---|
| The powers not **delegated** (given to) to the United States by the Constitution, nor **prohibited** (forbidden) by it to the states, are **reserved** (set aside) to the states respectively, or to the people.<br>*Source:* The Bill of Rights | 1. **What are delegated powers?** Delegated powers are powers given to the United States government by the Constitution.<br>2. **What powers are given to the states?** Powers given to the state are reserved powers. These are powers that have not been given to the U.S. government and are not forbidden to the states. |

| Document 7 The Nineteenth Amendment | Scaffolding Questions and Answers |
|---|---|
| The right of citizens of the United States to vote shall not be denied or **abridged** (limited) by the United States or by any state on the account of sex.<br><br>*Source:* The Bill of Rights | 1. **What is the purpose of the Nineteenth Amendment?** The purpose of the Nineteenth Amendment was to give women the right to vote.<br>2. **What group(s) was/were given the right to vote under the Nineteenth Amendment?** As a result of the Nineteenth Amendment, women were given the right to vote. |

## DOCUMENT-BASED QUESTION: THE AMERICAN REVOLUTION

| Document 1 The Royal Proclamation of 1763 | Scaffolding Questions and Answers |
|---|---|
| And we do further **declare** (state) it be our royal will and pleasure, for the present, as **aforesaid** (mentioned before), to reserve under our **sovereignty** (power), protection and **dominion** (control), for the use of the said Indian lands, all the land and territories not included within the limits of our said three new government (Quebec, East Florida and West Florida), or within the limits granted to the Hudson Bay Company; as also all of the land and territories lying to the westward of the sources of the rivers which fall into the sea from the west and the northwest as aforesaid.<br><br>Persons who have **inadvertently** (accidentally) settled upon such reserved lands to remove. No sale of Indian lands to be allowed, except to the Crown. The Indian trade to be free to English subjects, under license from the governor or commander in chief of some colony. Fugitives from justice, taking **refuge** (place of safety) in this reserved territory, to be **apprehended** (caught) and returned.<br><br>*Source:* HistoryCentral.com | 1. **According to the Royal Proclamation of 1763, what would happen to those considered fugitives?** According to the Royal Proclamation of 1763, those considered to be fugitives would be caught and returned to the colonies.<br>2. **How did the Royal Proclamation of 1763 restrict the rights of the Colonists?** The Royal Proclamation of 1763 restricted the rights of the colonists by not allowing them a choice in where they could settle. They could not purchase Indian lands or trade with the Indians unless they had a license from the governor. |

| Document 2 The Declaratory Act | Scaffolding Questions and Answers |
|---|---|
| That the said colonies and plantations in America have been, are, and of right ought to be, **subordinate** (inferior) unto, and dependent upon the imperial crown and parliament of Great Britain; and that the King's Majesty, by and with the advice and **consent** (agreement) of the lords spiritual and **temporal** (worldly), and commons of Great Britain, in parliament assembled, had, hath, and of right ought to have, full power and authority to make laws and statutes of sufficient force and validity, to bind the colonies and people of America, subjects of the crown of Great Britain, in all cases whatsoever. *Source:* HistoryCentral.com | 1. **How did the Declaratory Act increase Great Britain's power over the colonists?** The Declaratory Act increased Great Britain's power over the colonists by giving them the power and authority to make all laws for the colonists. 2. **How could this act lead to a violation of rights?** This act could lead to a violation of rights because the colonists were unable to make laws for themselves. The colonists had no way to overrule any law created by Great Britain. |

| Document 3 Paul Revere's Engraving | Scaffolding Questions and Answers |
|---|---|
|  *Source:* HistoryCentral.com | 1. **Which two groups are presented in the engraving?** The two groups presented in the engraving are the American colonists and the British soldiers. 2. **Which group is demonstrating an abuse of power? Why?** The group that is demonstrating an abuse of power is the British soldiers. They are shooting into a crowd of unarmed colonists. |

| Document 4 Colonial Legislation | | | Scaffolding Questions and Answers |
|---|---|---|---|
| *Act* | *Date* | *Effect on Colonists* | |
| Stamp Act | 1765 | All legal documents, newspapers, almanacs, playing cards, and dice were taxed. | 1. **How did these acts affect colonial life?** These acts affected colonial life by taxing products used by the colonists and eliminating colonial jobs. |
| Townshend Acts | 1767 | A tax was placed on lead, glass, paper, paint, and tea. British officers used writs of assistance to search and seize a ship's cargo if there was suspicion of smuggled goods. | 2. **How did the British attempt to control the amount of goods smuggled into the colonies?** The British attempted to control the amount of goods smuggled into the colonies by issuing writs of assistance, which allowed British officers to search and seize a ship's cargo if smuggling was suspected. |
| Tea Act | 1773 | British East India company sold tea directly to the colonists. Colonial tea merchants were eliminated from the tea trade. | |

| Document 5 The Intolerable Acts | Scaffolding Questions and Answers |
|---|---|
| 1. The port of Boston was closed to all trade until the colonists paid for the tea destroyed during the Boston Tea Party.<br>2. Colonists in Massachusetts could not hold town meetings more than once a year without the governor's permission.<br>3. British customs officials, as well as other British officials, charged with committing major crimes in the colonies would be tried in Great Britain, not Massachusetts.<br>4. A quartering act was passed forcing Massachusetts colonists to house British soldiers in their home.<br>*Source:* HistoryCentral.com | 1. **How did the Intolerable Acts punish the Massachusetts colonists for the Boston Tea Party?** The Intolerable Acts punished the Massachusetts colonists for the Boston Tea Party by closing the port of Boston until the colonists paid for the destroyed tea, limiting the amount of town meetings held in Massachusetts, allowing British officials accused of crimes to be tried in Great Britain, and forcing the colonists to provide shelter for British soldiers.<br>2. **How did these acts impact the economy of Massachusetts?** These acts impacted the economy of Massachusetts by closing the port of Boston. Trade could not take place in the colony of Massachusetts. Goods could not be imported or exported, thereby hurting the merchants who could not successfully run their businesses. |

| Document 6 | Scaffolding Questions |
| The Declaration of Independence | and Answers |

We hold these truths to be **self-evident** (easy to see), that all men are created equal; that they are **endowed** (given) by their **Creator** (God) with certain unalienable rights (rights that cannot be taken away); that among these are life, liberty, and the pursuit of happiness. That to **secure** (make safe) these rights, governments are **instituted** (established) among men, **deriving** (receiving) their just powers from the **consent** (permission) of the governed; that, whenever any form of government becomes destructive of these ends, it is the right of the people to alter or **abolish** (end) it, and to institute a new government, laying its foundation on such principles and organizing its powers in such form, as to them shall seem most likely to effect their safety and happiness.

*Source:* HistoryCentral.com

1. **According to the Declaration of Independence, where does the government get the right to rule?** According to the Declaration of Independence, the government gets its right to rule from the people it is governing.

2. **If the government does not listen to its people, what do the people have the right to do?** If the government does not listen to its people, the people have the right to abolish or get rid of the government and form a new government.

## DOCUMENT-BASED QUESTION: THE PROGRESSIVE ERA

| Document 1 | Scaffolding Qustions and Answers |

**Child Laborers in Indiana Glass Works, Midnight, Indiana. 1908.**

*Source:* The National Archives and Records Administration

1. **What are the children in the picture doing?** The children in the picture are working in the Indiana Glass Works factory.

2. **What dangers were these children exposed to while working in this factory?** These children were exposed to many different dangers such as operating dangerous machinery, working in unsafe and unsanitary conditions, and working long hours.

| Document 2 The Fifteenth Amendment | Scaffolding Questions and Answers |
|---|---|
| The right of citizens of the United States to vote shall not be denied or **abridged** (limited) by the United States or any state on account of race, color, or previous condition of servitude. *Source:* The Bill of Rights | 1. **What was the purpose of the Fifteenth Amendment?** The purpose of this amendment was to give African Americans the right to vote. 2. **How did this amendment change the lives of African Americans?** This amendment changed the lives of African Americans by giving them the legal right to have a say in government. |

| Document 3 The Eighteenth Amendment: Prohibition of Alcoholic Beverages | Scaffolding Questions and Answers |
|---|---|
| After one year from the **ratification** (approval) of this article the manufacture, sale, or transportation of intoxicating liquors within, the importation thereof into, or the exportation thereof from, the United States and all territory subject to the **jurisdiction** (authority) thereof for beverage purposes is hereby prohibited. *Source:* The Bill of Rights | 1. **What did the Eighteenth Amendment prohibit?** The Eighteenth Amendment prohibited the manufacture, sale, and transportation of alcohol. 2. **What impact did this amendment have on American society?** This amendment had a great impact on American life. Americans turned to bootlegging to get their alcohol. Speakeasies opened in many cities and towns and organized crime began to rise. |

| Document 4 | Scaffolding Questions and Answers |
|---|---|
| <br><br>*Sources:* The Library of Congress and www.library.ucla.edu/libraries/college/research/reference/images.htm | 1. **What are the women in the photograph asking for?** The women in the photograph are asking for suffrage, or the right to vote.<br><br>2. **Who are the women targeting in an effort to win suffrage?** The women are targeting the federal government, particularly President Wilson to help them gain suffrage. |

**Document 5**

**Legislative Acts of the Progressive Era**

**Scaffolding Questions and Answers**

| Act | Date | Explanation |
|---|---|---|
| Meat Inspection Act | 1906 | ensured clean conditions regarding meat processing; federal inspection of such facilities is required. |
| Pendleton Act | 1883 | Exams for federal jobs are now conducted by a civil service commission to fill jobs on the basis of merit. |
| Pure Food and Drug Act | 1906 | Labeling of food and drugs had to be truthful and accurate. |
| Sherman Anti-trust Act | 1890 | Monopolies and trusts were outlawed. |

1. **Which acts provided for ensuring the safety of food production?** The Meat Inspection Act and the Pure Food and Drug Act ensured the safety of food production.

2. **How did these legislative acts improve American society?** These acts improved American society by passing laws to make sure our food was safe to eat. Federal jobs would now be obtained on the basis of merit, making the process fair to all. Monopolies and trusts were outlawed providing fair competition in business.

| Document 6 The Nineteenth Amendment | Scaffolding Questions and Answers |
|---|---|
| The right of citizens of the United States to vote shall not be denied or **abridged** (limited) by the United States or by any state on the account of sex.<br><br>*Source:* The Bill of Rights | 1. **What was the purpose of the Nineteenth Amendment?** The purpose of the Nineteenth Amendment was to give women the right to vote.<br>2. **How did the Nineteenth Amendment change the role of women in American society?** The Nineteenth Amendment changed the role of women in American society by allowing women to have a voice in government. |

| Document 7 The Seventeenth Amendment | Scaffolding Questions and Answers |
|---|---|
| The Senate of the United States shall be composed of two Senators from each state, elected by the people thereof, for six years; and each Senator shall have one vote. The electors in each state shall have the qualifications **requisite** (requirement) for electors of the most numerous branch of the state legislatures.<br><br>*Source:* The Bill of Rights | 1. **How are U.S. Senators elected?** U.S. Senators are elected by the people of each state.<br>2. **How did this amendment give more power to the American people?** This amendment gave more power to the American people by allowing them to directly affect the law-making process. Americans could now see the candidate of their choice in office. |

## DOCUMENT-BASED QUESTION: THE CIVIL WAR

| Document 1 The Confederate Constitution, Section 9 | Scaffolding Questions and Answers |
|---|---|
| No **bill of attainder** (a legal act taking away a person's property if they are found guilty of a felony or treason), **ex post facto law** (a law imposing a punishment for an act that was legal at the time it was committed), or law denying or impairing the right of property in Negro slaves shall be passed.<br><br>*Source:* HistoryCentral.com | 1. **According to the Confederate Constitution, what position did a slave hold in American society?** According to the Confederate Constitution, a slave was considered to be the property of his master.<br>2. **How did Section 9 of the Confederate Constitution protect the institution of slavery?** This section of the Confederate Constitution protected the institution of slavery by stating that Negro slaves were considered property, which could not be taken away by any law. |

| Document 2<br>John C. Calhoun | Scaffolding Questions<br>and Answers |
|---|---|
| It may, in truth, be assumed as **maxim** (truth), that two races differing so greatly, and in so many respects, cannot possibly exist together in the same country, where their numbers are nearly equal, without one being **subjected** (under the control of) to the other. Experience has proved that the existing relation, in which the one is subjected to the other, in the slaveholding States, is consistent with the peace and safety of both, with great improvement to the **inferior** (not equal to); while the same experience proves that. . . . the **abolition** (end) of slavery would (if it did not destroy the inferior by conflicts, to which it would lead) reduce it to the extremes of **vice** (evil behavior) and **wretchedness** (meaness). In this view of the subject, it may be asserted, that what is called slavery is in reality a political institution, essential to the peace, safety, and **prosperity** (success) of those States of the Union in which it exists.<br><br>*Source:* HistoryCentral.com | 1. **What is John C. Calhoun's position on slavery?** John C. Calhoun believes that slavery is a political institution, which needs to exist.<br>2. **What does he believe will happen if slavery is abolished?** According to Calhoun, both races cannot live together peacefully. He believes that an end to slavery would lead to an end of peace in the slave states, and the African American race would be destroyed by internal conflicts. |

| Document 3 | Scaffolding Questions and Answers |
|---|---|

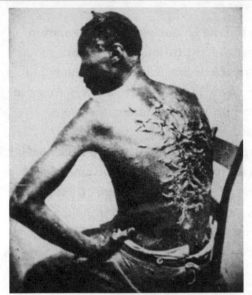

"Overseer Artayou Carrier whipped me. I was two months in bed sore from the whipping. My master come after I was whipped; he discharged the overseer. The very words of poor Peter, taken as he sat for his picture." Baton Rouge, LA, April 2, 1863.

*Source:* National Archives and Records Administration

1. **According to the photograph, how were slaves treated by their overseers?** According to the photograph, slaves were brutally treated by their overseers.
2. **How did the master of this slave react to this kind of treatment?** The master of this slave reacted to this kind of treatment by firing the overseer who whipped this slave.

| Document 4<br>The Declaration of Independence | Scaffolding Questions and Answers |
|---|---|

We hold these truths to be **self-evident** (easy to see), that all men are created equal; that they are **endowed** (given) by their **Creator** (God) with certain **unalienable rights** (natural rights which cannot be taken away); that among these are life, liberty, and the pursuit of happiness.

*Source:* HistoryCentral.com

1. **According to the Declaration of Independence, how are all men created?** According to the Declaration of Independence, all men are created equal.
2. **What rights are all men entitled to?** All men are entitled to their unalienable rights, such as life, liberty, and the pursuit of happiness.

| Document 5<br>The Emancipation Proclamation | Scaffolding Questions<br>and Answers |
|---|---|
| "And by virtue of the power and for the purpose **aforesaid** (mentioned before), I do order and **declare** (state) that all persons held as slaves within said **designated** (chosen) states (states fighting against the Union) and parts of states are, and **henceforward** (after this) shall be, free; and that the Executive Government of the United States, including the military and naval authorities thereof, will recognize and maintain the freedom of said persons.<br><br>And I hereby enjoin upon the people so declared to be free and **abstain** (withhold) from all violence, unless in necessary self-defense; and I recommend to them that, in all cases when allowed, they labor faithfully for reasonable wages.<br><br>And I further declare and make known that such persons, of suitable condition, will be received into the armed service of the United States to garrison forts, positions, stations, and other places, and to man vessels of all sorts in said service."<br><br>*Source:* HistoryCentral.com | 1. **How did the Emancipation Proclamation change the institution of slavery in America?** The Emancipation Proclamation changed the institution of slavery in America by freeing the slaves in states that were fighting against the Union.<br><br>2. **According to the Emancipation Proclamation, what was expected of the newly freed slaves?** Newly freed slaves were expected to work for reasonable wages, withhold from violence and when eligible, join the armed forces. |

## DOCUMENT-BASED QUESTION: WORLD WAR II

| Document 1<br>President Franklin D. Roosevelt | Scaffolding Questions<br>and Answers |
|---|---|
| We are now in this war. We are all in it—all the way. Every single man, woman and child is a partner in the most tremendous undertaking of our American history. We must share together the bad news and the good news, the defeats and the victories—the changing fortunes of war.<br><br>*Source:* HistoryCentral.com | 1. **According to President Roosevelt, who is involved in the war?** According to President Roosevelt, all Americans, including men, women, and children, are involved in the war.<br><br>2. **How will this war affect every American?** This war will affect every American by causing them to have both good and bad experiences. Americans will celebrate victories and agonize over defeats which result in the loss of loved ones. Every American will be forced to make sacrifices to help the war effort. |

| Document 2 | Scaffolding Questions and Answers |
|---|---|
| <br><br>*Source:* National Archives and Record Administration | 1. **Which group of Americans is this poster addressing?** This poster is addressing American women.<br><br>2. **According to the poster, how did the role of women change during World War II?** According to the poster, the role of women changed significantly during World War II. A woman's job was no longer solely in the home, but also in the workforce supporting the war effort. |

| Document 3<br>Radio Address of President<br>Franklin D. Roosevelt, October 12, 1942 | Scaffolding Questions and Answers |
|---|---|
| This whole nation of one hundred and thirty million free men, women, and children is becoming one great fighting force. Some of us are soldiers or sailors, some of us are civilians. Some of us are fighting the war in airplanes five miles above the continent of Europe or on the islands of the Pacific—and some of us are fighting in mines deep down in the earth of Pennsylvania or Montana. A few of us are decorated with medals for heroic achievement, but all of us can have that deep and permanent inner satisfaction that comes from doing the best we know how—each of us playing an honorable part in the great struggle to save our democratic civilization.<br><br>*Source:* HistoryCentral.com | 1. **According to the radio address, how were Americans helping the war effort?** According to the radio address, Americans were helping the war effort by directly participating as soldiers and sailors or indirectly participating by producing needed goods and providing valuable services.<br><br>2. **How would this effort preserve American democracy?** This effort would preserve American democracy by enabling America to successfully fight and win this war. |

| Document 4 | Scaffolding Questions |
| A Japanese Grocery Store | and Answers |

"Following evacuation orders, this store was closed. The owner, a University of California graduate of Japanese descent, placed the I AM AN AMERICAN sign on the storefront after Pearl Harbor." Oakland, CA, April 1942. Dorothea Lange.

*Source:* National Archives and Records Administration

1. **Why was this Japanese grocery store closed?** This Japanese grocery store was closed as a result of following evacuation orders. All American citizens of Japanese descent were placed in internment camps.

2. **Why was the sign, "I AM AN AMERICAN" placed on the storefront?** The sign, "I AM AN AMERICAN" was placed on the storefront to alert people to the fact that though the owner may have been of Japanese descent, he was an American citizen whose loyalty remained with the United States, and was in no way a supporter of Japan.

| Document 5 | Scaffolding Questions and Answers |

*Source:* National Archives and Records Administration

1. **What item in this photograph is being rationed?** The item being rationed in this photograph is tires because they were made of rubber. Rubber was essential to many products used during the war.

2. **Why would this product be rationed during World War II?** This product was rationed during World War II to produce necessary items to fight the war.

CHAPTER

# Document-Based Question Rubrics

The following rubrics coincide with the document-based essays and are to be used to estimate your score on an assessment exam. Remember, your score should be at least a three or higher.

| | | | | | | | |
|---|---|---|---|---|---|---|---|
| **5** | **Thoroughly** addresses **all** aspects of the task by accurately analyzing and interpreting at least **4** documents | Includes **accurate** and **relevant** information taken from the documents that explain the ways in which the U.S. Constitution protects or safeguards the rights of American citizens | Shows **additional** outside knowledge of the topic | Discusses **all** aspects of the task and **richly** supports the essay with accurate facts, examples, and details about the ways in which the U.S. Constitution protects the rights of American citizens | **Evenly** addresses **4** ways in which the U.S. Constitution protects or safeguards the rights of American citizens by **weighing** the importance, reliability, and validity of the evidence | Shows **excellent** organization by **weaving** the documents into the body of the essay | Includes a **strong** introduction and conclusion |
| **4** | Addresses **all** aspects of the task by **accurately** analyzing and interpreting at least **4** documents | Includes **mostly** accurate and relevant information that explains the ways in which the U.S. Constitution protects or safeguards the rights of American citizens, but discussion of the documents may be more **descriptive** than analytical | Shows **limited** outside knowledge of the topic | Supports the essay with **mostly** accurate facts, examples, and details about the ways in which the U.S. Constitution protects the rights of American citizens | Addresses **4** ways in which the U.S. Constitution protects or safeguards the rights of American citizens—**recognizes** that all evidence is not equally reliable and valid | Shows **good** organization in the body of the essay | Includes a **good** introduction and conclusion |
| **3** | Addresses **some** aspects of the task by **accurately** interpreting at least **3** documents | Includes **generally** accurate and relevant information that explains the ways in which the U.S. Constitution protects or safeguards the rights of American citizens—discussion of the documents may be more **descriptive** than analytical—**paraphrasing** of the documents may be present | Shows **little or no** useful outside knowledge of the topic | Supports the essay with **some** facts, examples, and details about the ways in which the U.S. Constitution protects the rights of American citizens—minimal factual **errors** may be present | Addresses **3** ways in which the U.S. Constitution protects or safeguards the rights of American citizens—**does not** always recognize that all evidence is not equally reliable and valid | Shows organization in the body of the essay | **Restates** the theme in the introduction and concludes with a **simple** restatement of the task |

| | | | | | | | |
|---|---|---|---|---|---|---|---|
| **2** | **Attempts** to address some aspects of the task but with **little** use of the documents | Includes **few** facts, examples and details of the ways in which the United States Constitution protects or safeguards the rights of American citizens—discussion may only **paraphrase** the contents of the documents | Has **no** useful or relevant outside knowledge of the topic | Essay includes factual **errors** about the way in that the U.S. Constitution safeguards the rights of American citizens | Addresses **less** than **3** ways in which the U.S. Constitution protects or safeguards the rights of American citizens— **does not** recognize that all evidence is not equally reliable and valid | Essay demonstrates a **poor** plan of organization and has many **flaws** | Introduction and conclusion is **extremely** weak |
| **1** | Shows **very limited** understanding of the task with **unclear** or **no** references to the documents | Facts, examples, and details of the ways in which the U.S. Constitution protects or safeguards the rights of American citizens are **not** present | Has **no** useful or relevant outside knowledge of the topic | Essay **mixes** accurate, inaccurate, and irrelevant information about the way in that the U.S. Constitution safeguards the rights of American citizens | **Does not** address or addresses in a **limited** way the ways in which the U.S. Constitution protects or safeguards the rights of American citizens— **does not** recognize that all evidence is not equally reliable and valid | Essay is **disorganized** and **unfocused** | **No** introduction or conclusion |
| **0** | Fails to address the task | Illegible | Blank paper | | | | |

## DBQ Rubric: The American Revolution

| | | | | | | | |
|---|---|---|---|---|---|---|---|
| **5** | **Thoroughly** addresses **all** aspects of the task by accurately analyzing and interpreting at least **4** documents | Includes **accurate** and **relevant** information taken from the documents that explains why colonists were justified in breaking away from Great Britain | Shows **additional** outside knowledge of the topic | Discusses **all** aspects of the task and **richly** supports the essay with accurate facts, examples, and details explaining why colonists were justified in breaking away from Great Britain | **Evenly** addresses **4** ways in which the colonists were justified in breaking away from Great Britain while **weighing** the importance, reliability, and validity of the evidence | Shows **excellent** organization by **weaving** the documents into the body of the essay | Includes a **strong** introduction and conclusion |
| **4** | Addresses **all** aspects of the task by **accurately** analyzing and interpreting at least **4** documents | Includes **mostly** accurate and relevant information that explains why colonists were justified in breaking away from Great Britain, but discussion of the documents may be more **descriptive** than analytical | Shows **limited** outside knowledge of the topic | Supports the essay with **mostly** accurate facts, examples, and details about why the colonists were justified in breaking away from Great Britain | Addresses **4** ways in which the colonists were justified in breaking away from Great Britain—**recognizes** that all evidence is not equally reliable and valid | Shows **good** organization in the body of the essay | Includes a **good** introduction and conclusion |
| **3** | Addresses **some** aspects of the task by **accurately** interpreting at least **3** documents | Includes **generally** accurate and relevant information that explains the ways in which the colonists were justified in breaking away from Great Britain—discussion of the documents may be more **descriptive** than analytical—**paraphrasing** of the documents may be present | Shows **little or no** useful outside knowledge of the topic | Supports the essay with **some** facts, examples, and details about the ways in which the colonists were justified in breaking away from Great Britain—minimal factual **errors** may be present | Addresses **3** ways in which the colonists were justified in breaking away from Great Britain—does **not** always recognize that all evidence is not equally reliable and valid | Shows organization in the body of the essay | **Restates** the theme in the introduction and concludes with a **simple** restatement of the task |

| 2 | **Attempts** to address some aspects of the task but with **little** use of the documents | Includes **few** facts, examples, and details of the ways in which the colonists were justified in breaking away from Great Britain—discussion may only **paraphrase** the contents of the documents | Has **no** useful or relevant outside knowledge of the topic | Essay includes factual **errors** about the way in which the colonists were justified in breaking away from Great Britain | Addresses **less** than **three** ways in which the colonists were justified in breaking away from Great Britain—**does not** recognize that all evidence is not equally reliable and valid | Essay demonstrates a **poor** plan of organization and has many **flaws** | Introduction and conclusion are **extremely** weak |
|---|---|---|---|---|---|---|---|
| 1 | Shows very **limited** understanding of the task with **unclear** or **no** references to the documents | Facts, examples, and details of the ways in which the colonists were justified in breaking away from Great Britain are **not** present | Has **no** useful or relevant outside knowledge of the topic | Essay **mixes** accurate, inaccurate, and irrelevant information about the ways in which the colonists were justified in breaking away from Great Britain | **Does not** address or addresses in a **limited** way the ways in which the colonists were justified in breaking away from Great Britain—**does not** recognize that all evidence is not equally reliable and valid | Essay is **disorganized** and **unfocused** | **No** introduction or conclusion |
| 0 | Fails to address the task | Illegible | Blank paper | | | | |

## DBQ Rubric: The Civil War

| 5 | Thoroughly addresses all aspects of the task by accurately analyzing and interpreting at least 3 documents | Includes accurate and relevant information taken from the documents that explains whether or not slavery was an acceptable form of labor in the South | Shows additional outside knowledge of the topic | Discusses all aspects of the task and richly supports the essay with accurate facts, examples, and details explaining whether or not slavery was an acceptable form of labor in the South | Evenly addresses 4 documents that explain whether or not slavery was an acceptable form of labor in the South, while weighing the importance, reliability, and validity of the evidence | Shows excellent organization by weaving the documents into the body of the essay | Includes a strong introduction and conclusion |
|---|---|---|---|---|---|---|---|
| 4 | Addresses all aspects of the task by accurately analyzing and interpreting at least 3 documents | Includes mostly accurate and relevant information that explains whether or not slavery was an acceptable form of labor in the South, but discussion of the documents may be more descriptive than analytical | Shows limited outside knowledge of the topic | Supports the essay with mostly accurate facts, examples, and details about whether or not slavery was an acceptable form of labor in the South | Addresses 4 documents that explain whether or not slavery was an acceptable form of labor in the South—recognizes that all evidence is not equally reliable and valid | Shows good organization in the body of the essay | Includes a good introduction and conclusion |
| 3 | Addresses some aspects of the task by accurately interpreting at least 2 documents | Includes generally accurate and relevant information that explains whether or not slavery was an acceptable form of labor in the South—discussion of the documents may be more descriptive than analytical—paraphrasing of the documents may be present | Shows little or no useful outside knowledge of the topic | Supports the essay with some facts, examples, and details about whether or not slavery was an acceptable form of labor in the South—minimal factual errors may be present | Addresses 3 documents which explain whether or not slavery was an acceptable form of labor in the South—does not always recognize that all evidence is not equally reliable and valid | Shows organization in the body of the essay | Restates the theme in the introduction and concludes with a simple restatement of the task |

| 2 | **Attempts** to address some aspects of the task but with **little** use of the documents | Includes **few** facts, examples, and details that explain whether or not slavery was an acceptable form of labor in the South—discussion may only **paraphrase** the contents of the documents | Has **no** useful or relevant outside knowledge of the topic | Essay includes factual **errors** about whether or not slavery was an acceptable form of labor in the South | Addresses less than **3** documents that explain whether or not slavery was an acceptable form of labor in the South—**does not** recognize that all evidence is not equally reliable and valid | Essay demonstrates a **poor** plan of organization and has many **flaws** | Introduction and conclusion are **extremely** weak |
| --- | --- | --- | --- | --- | --- | --- | --- |
| 1 | Shows very **limited** understanding of the task with **unclear** or **no** references to the documents | Facts, examples, and details that explain whether or not slavery was an acceptable form of labor in the South are **not** present | Has **no** useful or relevant outside knowledge of the topic | Essay **mixes** accurate, inaccurate, and irrelevant information about whether or not slavery was an acceptable form of labor in the South | **Does not** address or addresses in a **limited** way the explanation of whether or not slavery was an acceptable form of labor in the South—**does not** recognize that all evidence is not equally reliable and valid | Essay is **disorganized** and **unfocused** | **No** introduction or conclusion |
| 0 | Fails to address the task | Illegible | Blank paper | | | | |

| | | | | | | | |
|---|---|---|---|---|---|---|---|
| **5** | **Thoroughly** addresses **all** aspects of the task by accurately analyzing and interpreting at least **4** documents | Includes **accurate** and **relevant** information taken from the documents that explain the ways in which the Progressives attempted to reform American society | Shows **additional** outside knowledge of the topic | Discusses **all** aspects of the task and **richly** supports the essay with accurate facts, examples, and details explaining the ways in which the Progressives attempted to reform American society | **Evenly** addresses **4** documents that explain the ways in which the Progressives attempted to reform American society, while **weighing** the importance, reliability, and validity of the evidence | Shows **excellent** organization by **weaving** the documents into the body of the essay | Includes a **strong** introduction and conclusion |
| **4** | Addresses **all** aspects of the task by **accurately** analyzing and interpreting at least **4** documents | Includes **mostly** accurate and relevant information that explains the ways in which the Progressives attempted to reform American society, but discussion of the documents may be more **descriptive** than analytical | Shows **limited** outside knowledge of the topic | Supports the essay with **mostly** accurate facts, examples, and details about the ways in which the Progressives attempted to reform American society | Addresses **4** documents that explain the ways in which the Progressives attempted to reform American society—**recognizes** that all evidence is not equally reliable and valid | Shows **good** organization in the body of the essay | Includes a **good** introduction and conclusion |
| **3** | Addresses **some** aspects of the task by **accurately** interpreting at least **3** documents | Includes **generally** accurate and relevant information that explains the ways in which the Progressives attempted to reform American society—discussion of the documents may be more **descriptive** than analytical—**paraphrasing** of the documents may be present | Shows **little or no** useful outside knowledge of the topic | Supports the essay with **some** facts, examples, and details about the ways in which the Progressives attempted to reform American society—minimal factual **errors** may be present | Addresses **3** documents that explain the ways in which the Progressives attempted to reform American society—**does not** always recognize that all evidence is not equally reliable and valid | Shows organization in the body of the essay | **Restates** the theme in the introduction and concludes with a **simple** restatement of the task |

| 2 | **Attempts** to address some aspects of the task but with **little** use of the documents | Includes **few** facts, examples, and details that explain the ways in which the Progressives attempted to reform American society—discussion may only **paraphrase** the contents of the documents | Has **no** useful or relevant outside knowledge of the topic | Essay includes factual **errors** about the ways in which the Progressives attempted to reform American society | Addresses less than **3** documents that explain the ways in which the Progressives attempted to reform American society—**does not** recognize that all evidence is not equally reliable and valid | Essay demonstrates a **poor** plan of organization and has many **flaws** | Introduction and conclusion are **extremely** weak |
| --- | --- | --- | --- | --- | --- | --- | --- |
| 1 | Shows very **limited** understanding of the task with **unclear** or **no** references to the documents | Facts, examples, and details that explain the ways in which the Progressives attempted to reform American society are **not** present | Has **no** useful or relevant outside knowledge of the topic | Essay **mixes** accurate, inaccurate, and irrelevant information about the ways in which the Progressives attempted to reform American society | **Does not** address or addresses in a **limited** way the ways in which the Progressives attempted to reform American society—**does not** recognize that all evidence is not equally reliable and valid | Essay is **disorganized** and **unfocused** | **No** introduction or conclusion |
| 0 | Fails to address the task | Illegible | Blank paper | | | | |

| | | | | | | | |
|---|---|---|---|---|---|---|---|
| **5** | **Thoroughly** addresses **all** aspects of the task by accurately analyzing and interpreting at least **3** documents | Includes **accurate** and **relevant** information taken from the documents that explains the ways in which World War II changed American society | Shows **additional** outside knowledge of the topic | Discusses **all** aspects of the task and **richly** supports the essay with accurate facts, examples, and details explaining the ways in which World War II changed American society | **Evenly** addresses **4** documents that explain the ways in that World War II changed American society, while **weighing** the importance, reliability, and validity of the evidence | Shows **excellent** organization by **weaving** the documents into the body of the essay | Includes a **strong** introduction and conclusion |
| **4** | Addresses **all** aspects of the task by **accurately** analyzing and interpreting at least **3** documents | Includes **mostly** accurate and relevant information that explains the ways in which World War II changed American society, but discussion of the documents may be more **descriptive** than analytical | Shows **limited** outside knowledge of the topic | Supports the essay with **mostly** accurate facts, examples, and details about the ways in which World War II changed American society | Addresses **4** documents that explain the ways in which World War II changed American society—**recognizes** that all evidence is not equally reliable and valid | Shows **good** organization in the body of the essay | Includes a **good** introduction and conclusion |
| **3** | Addresses **some** aspects of the task by **accurately** interpreting at least **2** documents | Includes **generally** accurate and relevant information that explains the ways in which World War II changed American society—discussion of the documents may be more **descriptive** than analytical—**paraphrasing** of the documents may be present | Shows **little or no** useful outside knowledge of the topic | Supports the essay with **some** facts, examples, and details about the ways in which World War II changed American society—minimal factual **errors** may be present | Addresses **2** documents that explain the ways in which World War II changed American society—**does not** always recognize that all evidence is not equally reliable and valid | Shows organization in the body of the essay | **Restates** the theme in the introduction and concludes with a **simple** restatement of the task |

| | | | | | | |
|---|---|---|---|---|---|---|
| **2** | **Attempts** to address some aspects of the task but with **little** use of the documents | Includes **few** facts, examples, and details that explain the ways in which World War II changed American society—discussion may only **paraphrase** the contents of the documents | Has **no** useful or relevant outside knowledge of the topic | Essay includes factual **errors** about the ways in which World War II changed American society | Addresses less than **2** documents that explain the ways in which World War II changed American society—**does not** recognize that all evidence is not equally reliable and valid | Essay demonstrates a **poor** plan of organization and has many **flaws** | Introduction and conclusion are **extremely** weak |
| **1** | Shows very **limited** understanding of the task with **unclear** or **no** references to the documents | Facts, examples, and details that explain the ways in which World War II changed American society are **not** present | Has **no** useful or relevant outside knowledge of the topic | Essay **mixes** accurate, inaccurate, and irrelevant information about the ways in which World War II changed American society | **Does not** address or addresses in a **limited** way the ways in which World War II changed American society—**does not** recognize that all evidence is not equally reliable and valid | Essay is **disorganized** and **unfocused** | **No** introduction or conclusion |
| **0** | Fails to address the task | Illegible | Blank paper | | | | |

# *Pitfalls*

**D**id you ever plan a trip and forget a piece of luggage? Just when you think everything is going smoothly, something happens that gets you off track. Planning ahead and anticipating possible problems can help you avoid them. Often, essay writers fall into common traps like the following ones.

## ▶ PITFALL #1: DON'T FORGET TO WRITE A STRONG THESIS

One of the most important items to include in your first paragraph is a thesis statement. This statement must answer the task question and will become your essay guide. Without it, you will have no direction and nothing to prove in your document-based essay.

## ▶ PITFALL #2:
## BE SURE TO ANSWER THE TASK QUESTION

Sometimes you may not answer the question because you have interpreted it incorrectly. Be sure to slow down and carefully read each word of the directions and task question. Other times, even though you understand the question, you don't make clear connections to the question because you assume the reader understands your thoughts. Never assume that the reader understands the connections. You must make those connections for the reader by writing in a clear, logical order.

You may have written many document details, but if you don't answer the document question, then you have not succeeded in writing document-based essays. From time to time, reread your paragraphs. Ask yourself, "Does this statement answer some part of the task question?" If it doesn't, add details to make sure it does, or eliminate it.

## ▶ PITFALL #3:
## DON'T RAMBLE, ESPECIALLY WHEN ANSWERING SCAFFOLDING QUESTIONS

As you answer the scaffolding questions, quickly get to the point. Save the specific details for the actual essay because the essay is worth much more in the evaluation than the short answers. If you get off-task, you will waste valuable time and may not finish the actual document-based essay.

Be sure to stay focused and try not to become sidetracked. Writing many words does not necessarily make your writing more effective. Many times, numerous words for no particular reason can result in the reader misunderstanding your point. Try not to force the reader to **read between the lines.** Don't add needless information. Put every sentence to work and make every sentence count.

Remember:

- A sentence can introduce the background of a topic.
- A sentence that is a thesis statement can be one or more sentences.
- A sentence can provide a transition from one idea to the next.
- A sentence may be a topic sentence that states the main idea of the paragraph.
- A sentence can add a point.
- A sentence can make a comparison or a contrast.
- A supporting sentence gives support details and examples that prove the thesis.
- A sentence can state a cause or effect.
- A sentence can summarize and conclude the essay.

Make sure your sentences are doing one of these jobs. Otherwise, you run into the pitfall of rambling. Read your writing aloud to yourself. This may sound like a contradiction, but you can mouth the words. This will slow you down so that you can really see what you have written. You will be surprised how quickly you can catch errors by doing this exercise.

# ▶ PITFALL #4:
## AVOID TOO MANY DETAILS IN THE INTRODUCTION

Placing too many details in your introduction does not allow you to develop your topic in the body of the essay. This could lead to rambling and repetition. Introduce your major topics, but save the support details for the body.

Make sure that your introduction gets the reader's attention by generally introducing the topic in an interesting manner. You may include outside information here and put historical background information in your own words.

# ▶ PITFALL #5: UNDERSTAND KEY QUESTION WORDS

If you study the High Frequency Words starting on page 53 you will have a better understanding of task questions in general. This way you will actually answer what is being asked of you. For instance, if the task question says to describe certain events, then you have to explain these events. However, if the task question says to compare certain events, your writing will be more analytical because you will show the similarities and differences of these events.

# ▶ PITFALL #6: DON'T SIMPLY LIST FACTS

A simple listing of factual information will become a weak essay. You must write from a particular point of view and then relate the facts to each other. Also, you need to explain how these support facts relate to the thesis. This pitfall can be avoided by writing a strong thesis and effective topic sentences that support this thesis.

# ▶ PITFALL #7: AVOID OVERUSED OR EMPTY PHRASES

As you can see . . . It is obvious that . . . (nothing is obvious), I think . . . I believe. . . . my opinion . . . in conclusion . . . All of these are tired, overused, empty expressions that weaken rather than strengthen your writing. It is recommended that you read selections from the suggested reading list in Chapter 12. Reading well-written literature will give you effective models for your writing.

# ▶ PITFALL #8: DON'T CONTRADICT YOURSELF

Make sure that your introduction and your concluding opinions are the same. By reading and rereading your thesis and topic sentences, you can avoid this pitfall.

# ▶ PITFALL #9:
## USE THE THIRD PERSON POINT OF VIEW

There are three basic points of view from which a writer can write. The first person point of view is written about oneself, using the pronouns **I** and **me**. These pronouns and this point of view should be avoided when writing a DBQ because you are writing about historical events, not about your life.

The second point of view uses the pronouns **you** and **your** and is used when the writer is speaking directly to others. This point of view should also be avoided because you are not speaking directly to another person.

The third person point of view uses the pronouns **he, she, it,** and **they,** and is used to speak about someone or something else. This is the point of view you should use in your essays since you are speaking about someone or something from the past.

Since you are writing the essay, saying "I think" or "I believe" is redundant. Try to avoid using the first-person pronoun **I** or the second-person pronoun **you.** Stick with pronouns **he, she, they, one,** and only use these after full explanations for what **he, she, they, it,** and **one** represent.

# Recommended Reading List

Reading a wide variety of books makes you an informed reader. By becoming an informed reader, you will also become a more effective writer. We invite you to read as many historical fiction and nonfiction books as you can. The sooner you begin expanding your reading selections, the better. This will help you make connections between historical events and will truly help you to **read between the lines** of historical documents.

The following is a list of fiction and nonfiction books that covers early American history, including the Colonial period, the American Revolution, the New Nation, the Civil War, and the Progressive movement. It is our hope that by reading many of the fiction and nonfiction selections below, you will gain an appreciation and understanding of the historical events, settings, and people that have shaped our country.

*A Young Portrait: The American Revolution as Experienced by One Boy* by Jim Murphy. Houghton Mifflin (1998).

*Abe Lincoln: Log Cabin to White House* by Sterling North. Landmark Books (1987).

*Across Five Aprils* by Irene Hunt. (Newberry Honor Book) Berkley Publishing Group (1991).

*Amistad Rising: The Story of Freedom* by Veronica Chambers. Harcourt (1998).

*Amistad: A Long Road to Freedom* by Walter Dean Myers. Dreamworks (1998).

*And Then What Happened, Paul Revere?* by Jean Fritz. Paper Star (1996).

*April Morning* by Howard Fast. Bantam/Domain (1983).

*Autobiography of Benjamin Franklin* by Benjamin Franklin. Leonard W. Labaree. Yale University Press (1964).

*Behind Rebel Lines: The Incredible Story of Emma Edmonds, Civil War Spy* by Seymour Reit. Gulliver Books (2001).

*Beyond The Burning Time* by Kathryn Lasky. Point (1996).

*Black Rebellion: Five Slave Revolts* by Thomas Wentworth. Higginson, James M. McPherson (1998).

*Boston Tea Party: Rebellion in the Colonies* (Adventures in Colonial America) by James E. Knight. Troll Association (1998).

*Boys War: Confederate and Union Soldiers Talk About the Civil War* by Jim Murphy. Clarion Books (1993).

*Bull Run* by Paul Fleishman. Harper Trophy (1995).

*Can't You Make Them Behave, King George* by Jean Fritz. Paper Star (1996).

*Cast Two Shadows: The American Revolution in the South* by Ann Rinaldi. Gulliver Books (1993).

*Charlie Skedaddle* by Patricia Beatty. Troll Association (1989).

*Daughter of Liberty: A True Story of the American Revolution* by Robert M. Quakenbush. Hyperion Press (1999).

*Dear Ellen Bee: A Civil War Scrapbook of Two Union Spies* (My America Series) by Mary E. Lyons and Muriel M. Branch. Scholastic Inc. (2000).

*Don't Know Much About History: Everything You Need to Know about American History but Never Learned* by Kenneth C. Davis. Avon Books (1999).

*Don't Know Much About the Civil War: Everything You Need to Know About America's Greatest Conflict but Never Learned* by Kenneth C. Davis. Avon Books (1999).

*Don't Know Much About Geography* by Kenneth C. Davis. Avon Books (1999).

*Early Thunder* by Jean Fritz. Viking Press (1987).

*Finishing Becca: A Story About Peggy Shippen and Benedict Arnold* by Ann Rinaldi. Gulliver Books (1994).

*Five Smooth Stones: Hope's Diary, Philadelphia, Pennsylvania* (My America Series) by Kristina Gregory. Scholastic Trade (2001).

*Freedom's Wings: Corey's Diary, Kentucky to Ohio, 1857* (My America Series) by Sharon Dennis. Wyeth (2001).

*Get On Board: The Story of the Underground Railroad* by Jim Haskins. Scholastic (1993).

*Gettysburg* by MacKinlay Kantor. Landmark Books (1987).

*Give Me Liberty: The Story of the Declaration of Independence* by Russell Freedman. Scholastic Inc. (2000).

*Go Free or Die: A Story about Harriet Tubman* by Jeri Ferris. Carolrhoda Creative Minds Books (1989).

*Harriet Tubman: Conductor on the Underground Railroad* by Ann Petry. HarperTrophy (1996).

*Harriet Tubman: The Moses of Her People* by Sarah Bradford and Butler A. Jones. Lyle Stuart (1974).

*If You Lived at the Time of the American Revolution* by Kay Moore. Scholastic Trade (1998).

*If You Lived in Colonial Times* by Ann McGovern. Scholastic Trade (1992).

*If You Lived at the Time of the Civil War* by Kay Moore. Scholastic Trade (1994).

*If You Grew up with Abraham Lincoln* by Ann McGovern. Scholastic Trade (1976).

*If You Grew up with George Washington* by Ruth Belov. Scholastic Trade (1993).

*If You Were There When They Signed the Constitution* by Elizabeth Levy. Scholastic Trade (1992).

*If You Sailed on the Mayflower in 1620* by Ann McGovern. Scholastic Trade (1993).

*If You Traveled on the Underground Railroad* by Ellen Levine. Scholastic Trade (1993).

*Jamestown: New World Adventure* (Adventures in Colonial America) by James E. Knight. Troll Association (1999).

*Johnny Tremain* (Newbery Medal) by Esther Forbes. Yearling Books (1987).

*Journey to Monticello: Traveling in Colonial Times* (Adventures in Colonial America). Troll Association (1999).

*Lincoln: A Photobiography* (Newbery Medal) by Russell Freedman. Houghton Mifflin (1989).

*Molly Pitcher Young Patriot* by Augusta Stevenson. Alladin Paperbacks (1986).

*My Brother Sam is Dead* by James Lincoln Collier and Christopher Collier. Scholastic Paperbacks (1989).

*My Name is Not Angelica* by Scott O'Dell. Yearling Books (1990).

*Narrative of the Life of Frederick Douglass, an American Slave* by Frederick Douglass, Houston A. Baker, Jr. (Ed). Penguin American Library (1982).

*Nightjohn* by Gary Paulsen. Laurel Leaf (1995).

*Night Journeys* by Avi. Avon Camelot Books (2000).

*Paul Revere's Ride* by Henry Wadsworth Longfellow, Ted Rand (illustrator). Puffin (1996).

*Red Cap* by G. Clifton Wisler. Puffin (1994).

*Roll of Thunder, Hear My Cry* (Newberry Medal) by Mildred D. Taylor. Puffin (1997).

*Sarah Bishop* Scott O'Dell. Point (1991).

*Shades of Gray* by Carolyn Reeder. Alladin Paperbacks (1999).

*Sing Down The Moon* By Scott O'Dell. Laurel Leaf (1999).

*Silent Thunder: A Civil War Story* by Andrea Davis Pinkney. Scholastic Incorporated (1999).

*Stealing Freedom* (The Underground Railroad) by Elisa Carbone. Dell Yearling (1998).

*Streams to the River, River to the Sea* by Scott O'Dell. Fawcett Books (1988).

*Susan B. Anthony: Champion of Women's Rights* by Helen Albee Monsell, Al Fiorentino (illustrator). Alladin Paperbacks (1986).

*The American Revolution* by Bruce Bliver. Random House (1987).

*The American Revolution: A History* by Gordon S. Wood. Modern Library Chronicles (2002).

*The Autobiography of Benjamin Franklin* by Benjamin Franklin. Dover Thrift (1996).

*The Captive* by Scott O'Dell. Houghton Mifflin (1979).

*The Declaration of Independence and the Constitution of the United States: With Index by Pauline Maier.* Bantam Classic (1998).

*The Fifth of March: A Story of the Boston Massacre* by Ann Rinaldi. Gulliver (2000).

*The Fighting Ground* by Avi. Harper Trophy (1987).

*The First American: The Life and Times of Benjamin Franklin* by H.W. Brands. Anchor Books (2002).

*The Forgotten Heroes: The Story of the Buffalo Soldiers* by Clinton Cox. Point (1996).

*The Ideas of the Woman Suffrage Movement, 1890–1920* by Aileen S. Kraditor. W.W. Norton and Company (1981).

*The Journal of Douglas Allen Deeds: The Donner Party Expedition, 1846* (My Name is America Series) by W.R. Philbrick. Scholastic Trade (2000).

*The Journal of Jesse Smoke: A Cherokee Boy, Trail of Tears, 1838* (My Name is America Series) by Joseph Bruchac. Scholastic Trade. (2001).

*The Last Silk Dress* by Ann Rinaldi. Laurel Leaf (1999).

*The Narrative of Sojourner Truth* by Olive Gilbert. Dover Thrift (1997).

*The Pioneers Go West* by George Rippey Stewart. Random House (1997).

*The Red Badge of Courage* by Stephen Crane. Tor Books (1997).

*The Secret of Sarah Revere* by Ann Rinaldi. Gulliver Books (1995).

*The Secret Soldier: The Story of Deborah Sampson* by Ann McGovern. Scholastic Trade (1999).

*The Serpent Never Sleeps: A Novel of Jamestown and Pocahontas* by Scott O'Dell. Juniper (1990).

*The Slave's Narrative* by Charles T. Davis. Oxford University Print (1991).

*The Story of Harriet Tubman, Conductor of the Underground Railroad* by Kate McMullan. Yearling Books (1991).

*The Starving Time: Elizabeth's Diary; Book Two, Jamestown, Virginia, 1609* (My America Series) by Pauline Hermes. Scholastic Trade (2001).

*The True Confessions of Charlotte Doyle* by Avi. Avon (1992).

*The Underground Railroad: Life on the Road to Freedom* by Ellen Hanen. Discovery Enterprises, Ltd. (1999).

*The Winter at Valley Forge: Survival and Victory* (Adventures in Colonial America) by James E. Knight. Troll Association (1999).

*The Witch of Blackbird Pond* by Elizabeth George Speare (Newbery Medal). Laurel Leaf (1978).

*The Village: Life in Colonial Times* (Adventures in Colonial America) by James E. Knight. Troll Association (1998).

*Time Enough for Drums* by Ann Rinaldi. Laurel Leaf (2000).

*Thunder Rolling in the Mountains* by Scott O'Dell. Yearling Books (1993).

*To Be A Slave* by Julius Lester (Newbery Honor Book). Puffin (2000).

*Toliver's Secret* by Esther Wood-Brady. Random House (1993).

*Traitor: The Case of Benedict Arnold* (Unforgettable Americans) by Jean Fritz. Paper Star (1997).

*Turn Homeward, Hannalee* by Patricia Beatty Beech. Tree Books (1999).

*Undying Glory: The Story of the Massachusetts 54th Regiment* by Clinton Cox. Econo-Clad Books (1999).

*Up from Slavery* by Booker T. Washington. Dover Thrift Editions (1995).

*War Comes to Willy Freeman* by James Lincoln Collier and Christopher Collier. Yearling Books (1987).

*Westward to Home: Joshua's Diary, The Oregon Trail, 1848* (My America Series) by Patricia Hermes. Scholastic Trade (2001).

*What's the Big Idea, Ben Franklin?* by Jean Fritz. Paper Star (1997).

*Where was Patrick Henry on the 29th of May?* By Jean Fritz. Paper Star (1997).

*Will You Sign Here, John Hancock?* by Jean Fritz. Paper Star (1997).

*Wolf by the Ears* by Ann Rinaldi. Point (1993).